Immersion Blender Recipes
Recipes

Cookbook

Effortless Blending - Delicious Smoothies, Soups, Sauces, and Desserts for Every Meal

By
Wendall Jackson

Copyright

Smoothies & Shakes

Soup & Stews

Spreads & Hummus

Sauces & Dips

Dressings

Quick and Easy Blended

Desserts

Chapter

Smoothies & Shakes

Soup & Stews

Spreads & Hummus

Sauces & Dips

Dressings

Quick and Easy Blended

Desserts

TABLE OF CONTENT

Introduction:

Welcome to the Immersion Blender Recipes Cookbook! I'm Wendall Jackson, and I'm thrilled to share a collection of 101 delicious recipes showcasing the immersion blender's versatility and convenience. Whether you're a busy professional, a home cook looking to expand your culinary skills, or love blended dishes' ease and efficiency, this book is designed with you in mind.

The immersion blender, a hand or stick blender, is a powerhouse tool that can change your cooking experience. This handy gadget makes blending a breeze, from silky smoothies and hearty soups to creamy sauces and delectable desserts. Gone are the days of transferring hot soups to a blender in batches or struggling to achieve the perfect consistency for your sauces. With the immersion blender, you can blend directly in your pots, pans, and bowls, saving time and reducing cleanup.

This cookbook contains a wide range of dishes that are divided into categories to fit every meal and occasion:

1. Smoothies & Shakes: Start your day with energizing smoothies and shakes packed with fruits, vegetables, and superfoods.
2. Soups & Stews: Discover comforting and nourishing soups and stews, perfect for any season.
3. Spreads & Hummus: Elevate your snacks and appetizers with flavorful homemade spreads and hummus.
4. Sauces & Dips: Create versatile sauces and dips to enhance any dish, from pasta to grilled vegetables.
5. Dressings: Whip fresh and zesty dressings to complement your salads and bowls.
6. Quick and Easy Blended: Find recipes that are quick to prepare yet big on taste, ideal for those busy weeknights.
7. Desserts: Indulge in a selection of sweet treats, from creamy puddings to frozen delights.

Every recipe is designed to showcase the distinct features of the immersion blender, guaranteeing that you make the most of this beautiful kitchen appliance. The ingredients are readily available and nutritious, and the step-by-step instructions are simple enough to follow even by inexperienced cooks.

This cookbook inspires you to experiment with your immersion blender and discover new favorites that will become staples in your kitchen. So, plug in your blender, and let's start blending our way to delicious meals!

Happy Blending!

Wendall Jackson

What is Immersion Blender?

An immersion blender, also known as a hand and stick blender, is a versatile kitchen tool designed for Blending, pureeing, and mixing ingredients directly in the prepared container. Unlike traditional blenders, which require ingredients to be transferred to a separate jug, the immersion blender can be submerged in pots, bowls, or even measuring cups, making it incredibly convenient and easy to use.

Key Features and Benefits of an Immersion Blender:

Design and Structure:

Handheld: The immersion blender is handheld, with a motor in the upper part and a blending blade at the bottom.

Compact and Lightweight: Its slim, compact design makes it easy to store and maneuver.

Interchangeable Attachments: Many models come with various attachments, such as whiskers, choppers, and frothers, increasing their versatility.
Ease of Use:

Direct Blending: You can blend ingredients directly in the pot or bowl, especially for hot soups, sauces, and stews.

Minimal Cleanup: Since there's no need to transfer contents to a separate blender jug, there are fewer dishes to wash.
Versatility:

Smoothies and Shakes: Effortlessly blend fruits, vegetables, and other ingredients to create smooth, consistent drinks.

Soups and Stews: Puree soups directly in the cooking pot for a creamy texture without the hassle of transferring hot liquids.

Spreads and Hummus: Perfectly blend ingredients to achieve the desired consistency for spreads and hummus.

Dressings: Emulsify dressings quickly and efficiently.

Desserts: Prepare various desserts with minimal effort, including puddings and frozen treats.

Power and Speed:

Variable Speed Settings: Many immersion blenders offer multiple speed setting allowing you to control the blending process precisely.

Powerful Motor: Despite its compact size, the immersion blender often has a powerful motor capable of handling harsh ingredients.

Safety Features:

Ergonomic Handle: This handle's comfortable design guarantees a firm grasp.

Safety Locks: Some models include safety locks to prevent accidental operation.

Applications in the Kitchen:

Cooking and Baking: Ideal for preparing batters, doughs, and more.

Healthy Eating: Great for making baby food, smoothies, and purees with fresh, healthy ingredients.

Quick Meals: Perfect for whipping swift, leisurely meals with minimal preparation and cleanup.

Overall, the immersion blender is an essential kitchen tool that combines convenience, versatility, and efficiency, making it a favorite among home cooks or professional chefs.

How to Use an Immersion Blender?

Using an immersion blender is straightforward and can make many kitchen tasks quicker and easier. Whether you're new to this versatile tool or looking to refine your technique, here's a step-by-step guideline on how to use an immersion blender effectively:

1. Assemble Your Blender

Check Attachments: Ensure you have the correct attachment for your task. Most immersion blenders come with a blending blade, but some models also include whisks or chopper attachments.

Attach the Blade: Securely attach the blending blade or chosen accessory to the motor body.

2. Prepare Your Ingredients

Cut into Smaller Pieces: Chop more prominent ingredients into more minor, even pieces for best results. This helps the blender work more efficiently and reduces strain on the motor.

Fill the Container: Place the ingredients into a tall, narrow container for Blending. Many immersion blenders come with a blending beaker, but you can use any tall container, pot, or mixing bowl.

3. Begin Blending

Submerge the Blade: Insert the immersion blender into the ingredients, ensuring the blade is fully submerged to avoid splatters.

Start Slowly: Begin blending slowly to prevent ingredients from splattering. Gradually increase the speed as needed.

Move the Blender: Use an up-and-down motion to blend the ingredients evenly. Move the blender around the container for larger volumes to thoroughly mix all ingredients.

4. Blend to Desired Consistency

Check the Texture: Periodically stop blending to check the consistency of your mixture. Blend some more until you get the look you want.

Adjust Speed: If your immersion blender has multiple speed settings, adjust them as needed to achieve the perfect blend.

5. Safety and Cleanup

Turn Off and Unplug: Once you're done Blending, turn off the immersion blender and unplug it from the power source.

Detach the Blade: Carefully detach the blending blade or accessory.

Clean the Blade: Rinse the blade attachment under running water immediately after use. For more rigid residues, use a brush and mild soap. Be cautious of the sharp blades.

Dry and Store: Allow the blade and motor body to dry completely before reassembling and storing.

Tips for Effective Blending

Avoid Overfilling: Refill your container sparingly, as this can lead to spills and uneven Blending.

Use the Right Container: Tall and narrow containers work best for immersion blending, minimizing splatter and allowing for more efficient Blending.

Blend in Pulses: Use short pulses to avoid overheating the motor for thicker mixtures.

Be Cautious with Hot Liquids: When blending hot soups or sauces, submerge the blender to prevent splattering and allow steam to escape safely.

Applications of an Immersion Blender

Smoothies & Shakes: Effortlessly blend fruits, vegetables, and ice for delicious smoothies and shakes.

Soups & Stews: Puree soups directly in the pot for a smooth, creamy texture without transferring hot liquids.

Sauces & Dips: Create smooth, lump-free sauces and dips quickly and easily.

Spreads & Hummus: Achieve the perfect consistency for homemade spreads and hummus.

Dressings: Emulsify dressings with ease for a smooth, well-blended result.

Desserts: Prepare puddings, batters, and other dessert mixtures efficiently.

An immersion blender can simplify many kitchen tasks, making it a valuable tool for any home cook. With these tips and techniques, you can make the most of your immersion blender and easily enjoy delicious, blended creations.

How to Clean an Immersion Blender?

Properly cleaning your immersion blender after each use is crucial to maintaining it is performance and longevity. Here's a step-by-step guide on how to clean your immersion blender efficiently and safely:

1. Unplug the Blender
Safety First: Always unplug the immersion blender from the power source before cleaning to avoid accidental operation.

2. Detach the Blade or Attachment
Remove the Blade: Detach the blending blade or any other attachment (like a whisk or chopper) from the motor body. Most models have a release button or twist mechanism to remove the attachment easily.

3. Rinse Immediately
Quick Rinse: Rinse the blade or attachment under warm running water immediately after use. This helps prevent food from drying and sticking to the blades.

4. Clean the Blade and Attachments
Soapy Water: Put warm, soapy water in a bowl or sink. Put the blade and any extensions in water and use a soft brush or sponge to scrub them gently. Watch out for the sharp blades.

For Stubborn Residue: If food is stuck, let the attachment soak for a few minutes before scrubbing. Avoid using abrasive pads that can damage the blades.

5. Clean the Motor Body
Wipe Down: Wipe the motor body with a damp cloth. Do not immerse the motor body in water or run it under the tap as it contains electrical components.

Avoid Liquid Exposure: Ensure no liquid enters the motor housing to prevent damage.

6. Dry Thoroughly

Air Dry: Let the blade and attachments air dry before reassembling or storing. This helps prevent rust and ensures they are ready for subsequent use.

Wipe Dry: Use a dry cloth to wipe down the motor body and any other dampened components during cleaning.

7. Reassemble and Store

Reattach Components: Reattach the blade or other attachments to the motor body once everything is dry.

Store Safely: Store your immersion blender in a dry place. Please keep it in a safe spot where the blades won't be damaged, and the motor body won't be exposed to moisture.

Tips for Maintaining Your Immersion Blender

Regular Cleaning: Clean the immersion blender immediately after each use to prevent food from hardening on the blades.

Avoid Dishwashers: Check the manufacturer's instructions regarding dishwasher safety. Some parts may be dishwasher safe, but it's often best to hand wash to maintain the blades' sharpness and condition.

Inspect Regularly: Periodically check the blades and attachments for any signs of wear or damage. Replace any parts as necessary to ensure optimal performance.

Use Gentle Cleaners: Avoid harsh chemicals or abrasive cleaning tools that can damage the immersion blender's components.

Following these steps, you can keep your immersion blender in top condition, ensuring it remains a reliable tool in your kitchen for years. Proper cleaning maintains its performance and ensures food safety and hygiene.

1. APPLE CRISP SMOOTHIE

Prep Time: 5 Minutes | Cook Time: 00 Minutes

Total Time: 5 Minutes | Serving: 1

Ingredients

- 1 apple
- 1/4 cup of organic oats
- 1/2 cup of coconut yogurt
- 1 tbsp maple syrup
- 1/4 tsp nutmeg pinch of cardamom
- 1/2 tsp vanilla extract
- 1 tbsp almond
- 1 tbsp ground flax meal
- 1 serving vanilla protein powder
- 1/3-1/2 cup of almond milk
- 1 tsp cinnamon

Instructions

1. Blend it all after adding the least amount of milk until it's smooth. More milk would help mix everything. Anything is up for change.

2. BANANA BERRY SMOOTHIE

Prep Time: 15 Minutes | Cook Time: 00 Minutes

Total Time: 15 Minutes | Serving: 3

Ingredients

- 1/4 cup of orange juice
- 1 cup of frozen mixed berries
- 1/2 cup of Greek vanilla yogurt
- 1 cup of almond milk
- 1 banana

Instructions

1. Make the mixture smooth by blending the yogurt, banana, berries, and juice with milk.
2. The S-bell blade and speed 2 should be used on an immersion blender with a blending jar. As soon as the mixture reaches the bottom of the jar, tilt it to the side and slowly pull it up while the blender is still running. Keep doing it until it's smooth.

3. STRAWBERRIES & CREAM OATMEAL SMOOTHIE

Prep Time: 5 Minutes | Cook Time: 00 Minutes

Total Time: 5 Minutes | Serving: 2

Ingredients

- 1 cup of strawberries
- 1/2 cup of oats
- 1 tbsp honey
- 1 cup of milk
- 1 tsp vanilla
- 1/2 cup of cottage cheese

Instructions

1. Blend the milk and oats using a blender until the texture is smooth.
2. Blend them in for the last few ingredients until the mixture is smooth.

4. RASPBERRY SMOOTHIE

Prep Time: 10 Minutes | Cook Time: 00 Minutes

Total Time: 10 Minutes | Serving: 2

Ingredients

- 1 cup of yogurt
- 1 cup of frozen raspberries
- 1/2 tsp vanilla extract
- 1/2 of an avocado
- 1 large banana
- 2 tbsp maple syrup

Instructions

1. Blend it in a immersion blender. It's best to feel cold.

5. EASY YOGURT FRUIT SMOOTHIE

Prep Time: 5 Minutes | Cook Time: 00 Minutes

Total Time: 5 Minutes | Serving: 1

Ingredients

2. 5-ounce Greek vanilla yogurt frozen
3. 3 large strawberries sliced
4. Splash of milk
5. 1/3 cup of fresh blueberries
6. 1/2 medium banana

Instructions

1. Combine the yogurt, banana, and berries using a regular or immersion blender. Next, slowly add milk until the mixture is the consistency you want. Place it in a glass after mixing it well, and enjoy.

6. STRAWBERRY SMOOTHIE

Prep Time: 5 Minutes | Cook Time: 00 Minutes

Total Time: 5 Minutes | Serving: 2

Ingredients

- 500 ml non-dairy milk
- 3 tbsp natural peanut butter
- 2 ripe bananas
- 1 tsp vanilla extract
- 2-3 soft dates
- 150 grams of frozen strawberries

Instructions

1. Use a blender to mix everything. Make it very smooth with a high-speed blender, then serve it immediately.
2. You should immediately serve strawberry banana smoothies because they don't keep well. If you want a creamier smoothie, you can freeze the bananas instead of the strawberries.

7. AVOCADO PEANUT BUTTER SMOOTHIE

Prep Time: 5 Minutes | Cook Time: 00 Minutes

Total Time: 5 Minutes | Serving: 2

Ingredients

- 1 1/2 cups of milk
- 1/2 cup of peanut butter
- 3 Tbs cocoa powder
- 1/2 medium avocado
- 2 Tbs honey

Instructions

1. Using a mixer, smooth out the peanut butter, cocoa powder, milk, honey, and avocado. Serve and Enjoy.

8. BAKED APPLE SMOOTHIE

Prep Time: 20 Minutes | Cook Time: 10 Minutes

Total Time: 30 Minutes | Serving: 2

Ingredients

- 2 small apples
- 5 ounce plain yogurt
- 1/2 tsp ground winter spices
- 1/2 tbsp butter
- 1/2 cup of apple juice

Instructions

1. Place the apple pieces in a bowl and cut them up.
2. Melt the butter and add the apples to a small saucepan. As you cook them, move them around so they get soft.
3. Add the apple juice and stir everything together over low heat until it's warm. Take it off the heat.
4. A immersion blender can all be used to make the apples smooth. Place a towel over your blender or food processor and make sure it has a way for air to escape. This will keep you from getting burned.
5. After adding the spices, mix the yogurt. Equal amounts should be put into two mugs. Apple slices and cinnamon sticks should be put on top right away.

9. CREAMY BANANA AVOCADO SMOOTHIE

Prep Time: 5 Minutes | Cook Time: 00 Minutes

Total Time: 5 Minutes | Serving: 1

Ingredients

- 1/2 banana
- 1 cup of spinach
- 1 tsp maple syrup

- 1 cup of almond milk
- 1 small avocado

Optional Toppings:

- 1 Tbsp cottage cheese
- 1 tsp honey

- 1 Tbsp granola

Instructions

1. Blend everything using a blender or big jar until it's smooth.
2. If you use an immersion blender in a big jar and then put a straw in it to drink it right away, you might not have to wash the jar as often, which is how I like to work with frozen foods.
3. You can thin it out with more milk or water to make it easier to drink.
4. You can drink it as a smoothie or mix it with other foods if you'd rather eat it with a spoon.

10. COCONUT PINEAPPLE SMOOTHIE

Prep Time: 5 Minutes | Cook Time: 00 Minutes

Total Time: 5 Minutes | Serving: 1

Ingredients

- 2 frozen bananas
- 1 cup of pineapple chunks

- Honey
- 1 cup of coconut milk

Instructions

1. Mix everything until it's smooth.

11. VANILLA MILKSHAKE

Prep Time: 5 Minutes | Cook Time: 00 Minutes

Total Time: 5 Minutes | Serving: 2

Ingredients

- Chocolate chips
- 1 Cups of milk
- Shot of Alcohol
- Whipped Cream
- Chocolate syrup
- 3 large scoops of ice cream

Instructions

1. Put the milk and ice cream in the 3-cup of container. Then, mix them with an immersion blender. Move more slowly at first and then faster up and down the mix. Add the alcohol now if you're going to do it.
2. Add chocolate syrup to a cold glass, then pour the drink in. You can put chocolate chips, whipped Cream, or sprinkles on top.
3. Remember to relax and enjoy your break.

12. PUMPKIN SPICE PROTEIN SMOOTHIE

Prep Time: 5 Minutes | Cook Time: 00 Minutes

Total Time: 5 Minutes | Serving: 1

Ingredients

- 2 tbsp vanilla protein powder
- 1/3 cup of pumpkin puree
- 1/2 tsp pumpkin pie spice
- 2 cups of unsweetened almond milk
- whipped Cream
- 1 frozen banana

Instructions

1. Use an immersion or a blender to blend everything in a jar. Add pumpkin pie spice and whipped Cream.

13. GREEN PROTEIN POWER BREAKFAST SMOOTHIE

Prep Time: 5 Minutes | Cook Time: 00 Minutes

Total Time: 5 Minutes | Serving: 2

Ingredients

- 1 cup of unsweetened almond milk
- 1-2 large handfuls of baby spinach
- ½ cup of chopped mango
- 1 ripe banana
- 2 tbsp hemp hearts
- ½ scoop vanilla protein powder
- ¼ cup of pumpkin seeds

Instructions

1. First, put the pumpkin seeds, then the hemp hearts, then the spinach, and finally the banana. Mix the almond milk and pumpkin seeds until they are very smooth. This recipe makes enough for two big smoothies.

14. STRAWBERRY BANANA MILKSHAKE

Prep Time: 10 Minutes | Cook Time: 00 Minutes

Total Time: 10 Minutes | Serving: 4

Ingredients

- 1 cup of milk
- 2 large bananas
- 26 ounce strawberries
- 2 tbsp sweetener honey
- 1 tsp vanilla extract

Instructions

1. Get the bananas and strawberries' tops off. Include your sweetener of choice and vanilla extract in the blender. Combine until it's smooth.

15. PALEO BANANA CHOCOLATE SHAKE

Prep Time: 10 Minutes | Cook Time: 00 Minutes

Total Time: 10 Minutes | Serving: 2

Ingredients

- 1 tbsp almond butter
- 1/2 cup of coconut milk
- 1/2 cup of cold water
- 2 frozen bananas
- Pinch of cinnamon
- 1.5tsp dark chocolate cocoa powder

Instructions

1. Put the things you want to make smooth into a blender or a large cup and blend them. You can add more water if you need to get the right consistency. Serve right away.

16. TOMATO BASIL SOUP

Prep Time: 10 Minutes | Cook Time: 25 Minutes

Total Time: 35 Minutes | Serving: 6

Ingredients

- ➢ 1 dash of Italian seasoning
- ➢ Salt & pepper
- ➢ 1 tbsp olive oil
- ➢ 2 tbsp butter
- ➢ 1 clove garlic
- ➢ 2 cans whole San Marzano tomatoes
- ➢ 1.5 cups of chicken
- ➢ 1 medium onion
- ➢ 1/2 cup of Heavy Cream
- ➢ 12 leaves fresh basil

Instructions

1. Add the onion, butter, and oil to the pot on medium-high heat. Let the onion cook for 5-7 minutes or until it turns brown.
2. Add the garlic and Italian seasoning after the tomatoes and chicken broth.
3. Increasing the heat should cause the soup to boil. Simmer it for 8 minutes with the lid slightly open after lowering the heat.
4. Using a blender, make the soup smooth if needed. Once the Cream and basil are mixed, add salt and pepper.

17. CREAMY BUTTERNUT SQUASH SOUP

Prep Time: 10 Minutes | Cook Time: 20 Minutes

Total Time: 30 Minutes | Serving: 6

Ingredients

- 1 tbsp minced garlic
- 1 green apple
- 1 red bell pepper
- 1 white onion
- 2 cups of vegetable
- ½ tsp smoked paprika
- 3 tbsp olive oil
- 1 large carrot
- ¼ tsp pepper
- 1 stalk celery
- 2 15-ounce cans of unsweetened coconut milk
- 1 tsp salt
- 3 pounds butternut squash

Instructions

1. Put the butternut squash, carrot, apple, bell pepper, garlic, onion, and celery in a large stockpot over medium-high heat. Add the olive oil and salt. After three to four minutes, the onions should be clear, and the garlic should smell heavenly.
2. Set the mixture on fire and add the stock, pepper, salt, and smoked paprika. Put the pan on medium heat for 5 to 10 minutes or until the squash and vegetables are very soft.
3. Include the milk from the coconut. Utilize an immersion blender to blend things until they are smooth. If you have a powerful blender, you can put small amounts at a time and blend until the mixture is smooth and creamy.
4. Optional: Add salt and pepper to taste. To make it thinner, add more water or stock. Style it however you like, then serve.

18. POTATO LEEK SOUP

Prep Time: 5 Minutes | Cook Time: 25 Minutes

Total Time: 30 Minutes | Serving: 6

Ingredients

- salt and fresh pepper
- 4 cups of chicken broth
- 1 tbsp flour
- 1 tbsp butter
- 2 medium russet potatoes
- 1/2 large white onion
- 4 medium leeks
- 1/2 cup of milk
- fresh chives for garnish

Instructions

1. Wash the leeks very well to get rid of any dirt. I usually cut them in half horizontally to keep them clean and separate the rings. Cut them up nicely after you wash them.
2. Add the flour & melted butter in a soup pot.
3. Put it together with a wooden spoon. This will make your soup thicker and taste better.
4. After you turn on the heat, add the potatoes, leeks, onion, and chicken broth.
5. Cover and cook on low warm for 20-25 minutes or until potatoes are soft.
6. Utilize an blender to make the soup smooth. Put in the milk, salt, and pepper to taste. Serve right away.

19. CARROT GINGER SOUP

Prep Time: 10 Minutes | Cook Time: 30 Minutes

Total Time: 40 Minutes | Serving: 4

Ingredients

- 1/2 tsp orange zest
- 4 tbsp butter
- 4 cups of chicken stock/broth
- 1.5 pounds carrots peeled

- 1 tbsp fresh ginger minced
- 1 yellow onion diced
- plain yogurt
- kosher salt

Instructions

1. In a large pot over medium to high heat, melt the four tbsp of butter. Stir the butter over and over until it turns brown and foams up.
2. Set the heat lower and add the onions. After two minutes, they should be soft. Lots of salt and carrots. Add more butter and cook for three to five minutes until the carrots become soft.
3. Include the chicken stock, chopped ginger, and orange zest. Start by boiling it. After that, cover it and set the heat to low for 20 minutes.
4. Don't heat it anymore. An immersion blender lets you create any smoothness you desire in the soup.
5. Tasting it will help you decide if it needs more salt. Feel free to serve the soup hot or cold. Before you serve it, it should be chilled for about two hours. Put plain yogurt, fresh basil, green onions, or herbs on top.

20. SPICY SWEET POTATO SOUP

Prep Time: 10 Minutes | Cook Time: 15 Minutes

Total Time: 25 Minutes | Serving: 7

Ingredients

- 1 tsp salt
- Cilantro or parsley
- 1 2-inch piece of ginger
- 1 tbsp red curry paste
- 3 tbsp lemon juice
- 1 15 ounce can of coconut milk
- 1 1/2 pounds, usually 3-4 sweet potatoes
- 3 cups of chicken
- 1 onion
- 1 tbsp olive oil

Instructions

1. Warm up the olive oil in a big stock pot over medium-low heat. It's time to cook the onions until they get soft. After you add the red curry paste, cook for one more minute.
2. Bring the broth and sweet potatoes to a boil. Let the sweet potatoes boil for 10 to 15 minutes or until they are soft enough to pierce with a fork. Put the soup in an immersion blender and blend it until smooth. Those who don't have an immersion blender can blend it in standing blenders in groups.
3. Mix well after adding salt, lemon juice, and coconut milk. Bring it to a slow boil, then cook for 5 to 10 minutes.
4. If you want, add fresh cilantro or parsley as a garnish.

21. CAULIFLOWER CHEESE SOUP

Prep Time: 5 Minutes | Cook Time: 20 Minutes

Total Time: 25 Minutes | Serving: 8

Ingredients

- ➤ 4 cloves Garlic
- ➤ 4 cups of Cauliflower
- ➤ 3 1/2 cups of Chicken broth
- ➤ 3 cups of Cheddar cheese
- ➤ 1 cup of Heavy Cream

Instructions

1. In a Dutch oven, cook garlic for one minute over medium heat until it smells good.
2. Heavy Cream, chicken broth, and chopped cauliflower should all be added. Cut the heat down when it starts to boil. Let it cook slowly for 10 to 20 minutes until the cauliflower is soft.
3. Take out about a third of the cauliflower pieces with a slotted spoon. Put them away.
4. The soup should be smooth if you use an immersion blender with the rest of the cauliflower.
5. Lower the heat. Add the shredded cheddar cheese slowly, stirring all the time, 1/2 cup at a time, until it melts. Puree it again to make it smooth.
6. Take it off the heat. It's time to add the cauliflower florets you saved back to the soup.

22. VEGETARIAN MUSHROOM SOUP

Prep Time: 10 Minutes | Cook Time: 30 Minutes

Total Time: 40 Minutes | Serving: 4

Ingredients

- 3 cups of low-sodium vegetable broth
- 1/4 tsp thyme
- Salt and pepper
- 2 cloves garlic
- 1/2 cup of evaporated milk
- Fresh thyme
- 1 large onion
- 2 tbsp butter
- 1 pound baby bella mushrooms
- 2 tsp soy sauce
- 1 tbsp olive oil
- 1/4 cup of all-purpose flour

Instructions

1. Slowly melt the olive oil and butter in a big pot or Dutch oven.
2. About 4 minutes later, add the chopped onions and cook them until they turn clear.
3. Incorporate chopped garlic and mushroom slices. Wait 8 to 10 minutes until the mushrooms are soft and have given off their water.
4. After adding the flour, cook for two minutes.
5. Combine the soy sauce and vegetable broth, then bring the whole thing to a simmer. Wait another 10 to 15 minutes.
6. Remove from the heat and put the evaporated milk, stirring it in.
7. Blend the soup with an immersion blender until it's the right consistency. Put in 2 cups of soup and blend until it's smooth if you don't have an immersion blender. Put it back in the soup pot now.
8. Taste the food before you serve it and make any necessary changes to the seasoning. Add a little salt, soy sauce, or both if you think it needs more salt.

23. CREAMY BROCCOLI CHEDDAR SOUP

Prep Time: 25 Minutes | Cook Time: 10 Minutes

Total Time: 35 Minutes | Serving: 6

Ingredients

- 4 cups of chicken stock
- 1/4 tsp grated nutmeg
- 8 ounces grated sharp cheddar cheese
- 1/4 cup of melted butter
- 16 ounce fresh frozen broccoli florets
- 1 cup of grated carrot
- 2 1/2 cups of half-and-half
- 1 tbsp melted butter
- Kosher salt
- 1/4 cup of flour
- 1/2 medium chopped onion

Instructions

1. In a large size pot over medium to high heat, melt the butter. Put the onion and cook for about three minutes, until it gets soft. Add more butter and flour and whisk for three to five minutes to make a roux. As you add the half-and-half and chicken stock, whisk the mixture. Let it cook for 20 minutes.
2. Add the broccoli florets and grated carrot and mix them in. Put in some nutmeg, salt, and pepper. Let it cook slowly for 30 to 35 minutes.
3. Take the soup off the heat & use an immersion blender to make it smooth.
4. Add cheddar cheese and stir. Then, turn the heat back down to low. Let it cook for 10 minutes, then serve.
5. Have fun!

24. RICH AND CREAMY CLASSIC LOBSTER BISQUE

Prep Time: 15 Minutes | Cook Time: 50 Minutes

Total Time: 1 Hour 5 Minutes | Serving: 5

Ingredients

- 3 tbsp tomato paste
- 2 bay leaves
- 3 cloves garlic
- 1 cup of half and half
- 1 cup of white wine
- 1/2 tsp pepper
- 4 tbsp butter
- 3 tbsp flour
- 1/4 cup of brandy
- 1/2 tsp dried tarragon

- 1 tsp salt
- 1 large shallot
- 1 carrot
- 1 pound lobster tails
- 2 cups of seafood stock
- 1/2 tsp dried thyme
- 1 1/2 tsp Tabasco
- 1 tsp smoked paprika
- 1 rib celery

Instructions

1. Melt 2 tbsp of butter in a soup pot over medium heat.
2. Place the celery, carrot, and shallot in the pan and cook for three minutes.
3. Also, add smoked paprika, salt, pepper, and bay leaves and stir them in. Saute for two more minutes.
4. Put in the garlic and cook for one minute.
5. Put the tomato paste and stir it in. Cook until it melts and covers the vegetables.
6. Add the flour and mix it in until it's well mixed in.
7. Add the brandy and stir it in after taking the pan off the heat.
8. Put the wine and cook for one minute.
9. Add the seafood stock and stir.
10. Put tobasco sauce in. Bring the mix to a boil.
11. Lower the heat & let it simmer without cover for 10 minutes.
12. Meanwhile, take the lobster meat out of its shells and cut it into small pieces.
13. Cover the bisque and let it cook for 30 minutes with half of the lobster added.
14. Use an immersion or regular blender to blend the mixture in small amounts until it is very smooth.
15. Mix in the half-and-half, then bring it to a low boil.
16. Set the saute pan on low heat and melt the rest of the butter.
17. Cook the rest of the lobster until it's fully cooked.
18. Put lobster in each of 4 bowls and pour bisque over the top of each.
19. If you want, you can put chopped parsley as a garnish.

25. CHICKEN TORTILLA SOUP

Prep Time: 10 Minutes | Cook Time: 30 Minutes

Total Time: 40 Minutes | Serving: 4

Ingredients

- 3 cups of chicken stock
- 3-4 cloves garlic
- 1 onion
- kosher salt
- ¾ cup of black beans
- 1 cup of shredded rotisserie chicken
- ¼ tsp dried oregano

- ¼ tsp cumin
- 1 14-ounce can of roasted tomatoes
- ¾ cup of frozen corn
- 2 tsp olive oil
- 1 jalapeno pepper stem
- ½ tsp ground chipotle pepper

Toppings:

- shredded cheese
- quartered limes
- sliced jalapenos
- 2 small corn tortillas

- sliced green onions
- cubed avocado
- cilantro

Instructions

1. Set a big pot on medium-high heat. Put in the jalapeno, onion, and garlic. Saute until the onion turns clear and the jalapeno gets soft. Add the dried oregano, cumin, salt, and chipotle pepper to taste. Mix it all, then cook for one to two minutes until the spices brown.
2. The fire-roasted tomatoes and chicken stock should be added, and the whole thing should be brought to a boil. Bring it down to a simmer and leave it there for 30 minutes.
3. Using an immersion blender, blend the soup ingredients until the soup is smooth. Add more salt and pepper if you think it's needed. Add corn, black beans, and chicken shreds.
4. Place some soup in each of 4 bowls. Add cheese, avocado, cilantro, and crispy tortilla strips to each bowl. If you want, you can add more lime juice or Jalapeno slices. Serve right away.
5. In a small size skillet, heat the vegetable oil over medium-high heat. This will help you make the strips of tortilla. Add the tortilla strips all at once to the hot oil. Flip them over once during the 30 to 45 seconds of quick frying to make sure both sides get crispy. When the tortillas are crisp, use tongs to remove them from the pan and place them on a plate lined with paper towels to dry.

26. SPICY ROASTED VEGETABLE SOUP

Prep Time: 20 Minutes | Cook Time: 20 Minutes

Total Time: 40 Minutes | Serving: 12

Ingredients

- 1 tomato
- 1 tsp freshly ground black pepper
- 1 eggplant
- 1/2 tsp ground cumin
- 2 carrots
- 2 yellow summer squash
- Grated Pecorino
- 1 green bell pepper
- 1/4 tsp ground cinnamon
- 1/4 tsp ground turmeric
- 1/2 tsp ground coriander
- 1 tsp salt
- 1/2 large onion
- 2 large jalapeno peppers
- 5 cups of chicken
- 3 tsp coconut oil
- 1/2 cup of Heavy Cream

Instructions

1. Warm the oven up to 425°F. Aluminum foil, parchment paper, or silicone mats should line two baking sheets with edges.
2. Put the vegetables in a big bowl and mix them. After that, put in the pepper, salt, and coconut oil. Cover all of the vegetables by tossing them. Place the vegetables that have already been prepared on the baking sheets. The vegetables should be roasted for 30 minutes, stirring them now and then until they are soft and golden.
3. Take it out of the oven and put it in a big pot on the stove. Set the pot on medium-low heat and add the broth and spices. Let it cook for another 20 minutes.
4. Take it off the heat. Blend until smooth with an immersion blender. Add Cream and stir. Add more broth or Cream if you want to change the consistency. Add pepper and salt to taste.
5. Pour into bowls, decorate with extras, and serve hot.

27. THAI COCONUT CURRY CARROT SOUP

Prep Time: 15 Minutes | Cook Time: 40 Minutes

Total Time: 55 Minutes | Serving: 6

Ingredients

- ➢ 2 Tbsp butter
- ➢ 1 sweet potato
- ➢ salt and pepper
- ➢ 1 yellow onion
- ➢ 1 pound. carrots
- ➢ 4 Tbsp red Thai curry paste
- ➢ 3 cups of vegetable broth
- ➢ 1 13.5ounce. can full-fat coconut milk

Instructions

1. Cut the onion into small pieces and put them in a big pot with the butter. The onion should be cooked until it is soft and clear.
2. The Thai curry paste should be added after the onions are soft. Saute for another minute or so.
3. Peel and cut up the sweet potato while the onion cooks. Once the curry paste is cooked, put the sweet potato to the pot. Keep cooking the sweet potatoes while you peel and slice the carrots. Put the carrot slices into the pot as you make them.
4. Put the lid on the pot and raise the heat to medium-high. Add the vegetable broth and stir it in. The soup should first boil, then the heat should be low. Let it simmer for 30 minutes, stirring now and then. The carrots and sweet potatoes should be so soft after 30 minutes that they should fall apart when you stir the pot.
5. To help it cool down, turn off the heat and take the pot off the hot stovetop. Put the coconut milk and mix it in. You can save one or two tbsp of coconut milk to sprinkle on top of the soup when it's done.
6. You can either wait for the soup to cool down more or use a regular blender in small amounts to blend it better. Once the soup is smooth, you can taste it and add salt or pepper. You can put Sriracha sauce and fresh cilantro on top if you want to.

28. CREAMY PARSNIP AND APPLE SOUP

Prep Time: 15 Minutes | Cook Time: 55 Minutes

Total Time: 1 Hour 10 Minutes | Serving: 6

Ingredients

- 5 cup of unsweetened Cashew Milk
- 2 tsp curry powder
- sea salt and black pepper
- 3 Granny Smith apples
- 1 tsp ground coriander
- 6 cups of vegetable broth
- 1 tsp ground cumin
- 0.5 cup of yellow onion
- 1 medium potato
- 5 parsnips
- 2 tbsp olive oil
- fresh chives

Crustini – Optional:

- 1 baguette
- ¼ cup of olive oil

Instructions

1. In a big size Dutch oven, heat the olive oil over medium heat.
2. After you add the onion, cook for three to five minutes or until it gets soft but not brown.
3. Mix the apples, potatoes, and parsnips after adding them.
4. Put the pan under a lid and turn down the heat. Cook until the apples begin to break up. If you stir it occasionally, this should take about 10-12 minutes.
5. Spices like cumin, coriander, salt, and pepper should be added. Bring up the temperature.
6. Lower the heat, put the lid back on the pan, and let it simmer for 35 to 40 minutes or until the vegetables are soft.
7. Use an immersion blender to blend the soup until it is smooth. Put some of it into a blender at a time and blend until smooth. Then, add it back to the pan.
8. Add the cashew milk and taste to see if the seasonings need to change.
9. To serve, put the soup into shallow bowls. If you want, add two crustini and sprinkle chives on top.

Optional Crustini:

1. Warm up the broiler. Eight to ten half-inch baguette slices should be cut and dripped with olive oil.
2. Toast the slices on a pan lined with foil, about 4 inches from the heat. Flip them over so that both sides get a little toasted.

29. MEXICAN CHICKEN SOUP

Prep Time: 15 Minutes | Cook Time: 30 Minutes

Total Time: 45 Minutes | Serving: 6

Ingredients

- 1/2 tsp smoked paprika
- 1.25pounds boneless chicken thighs
- 1 tbsp olive oil
- 2 tsp cumin
- 1 yellow onion
- 1/4 tsp ground black pepper
- 1/2 cup of freshly chopped cilantro leaves

- 1 jalapeno
- 2 tsp sea salt
- 3 carrots
- 3 cups of water
- 4 cloves garlic
- 2 celery ribs
- 1 can fire-roasted diced tomatoes
- 1/2 tsp dried oregano

Instructions

1. In a big pot over medium-high heat, add the olive oil. Add the onion, celery, and carrots. Cook for about 8 minutes or until the vegetables start to soften. Add the smoked paprika, cumin, oregano, and Jalapeno this time. Stir for one more minute.
2. Add chicken, diced tomatoes, salt, black pepper, and water. slower the heat and cover the pot if the water begins to boil. It should be done in 15 to 20 minutes. Employ a meat thermometer to confirm that the meat's internal temperature reaches 165ºF.
3. Put the chicken out of the pan with tongs on a plate. After some time, use two forks to shred the chicken. Mix in the fresh cilantro before adding the chicken back in, and use an immersion blender to slowly puree the soup until it reaches the texture you want.
4. Add the chicken back to the soup and taste to see if it needs more seasoning. Add an extra tsp of salt, but start by adding only half a tsp at a time to make sure you don't add too much. Immediately serve hot with any toppings you like. Food you don't want to eat can be kept in the fridge for up to four days in an airtight container.

30. QUINOA PEA SOUP

Prep Time: 5 Minutes | Cook Time: 25 Minutes | Total Time: 30 Minutes | Serving: 6

Ingredients

- 1/2 tsp salt
- 1 medium onion
- 1/4 tsp black pepper
- 2-1/2 cups of frozen green peas
- 1 cup of water
- 1/2 cup of quinoa
- 2 tsp canola oil
- 2 cans low sodium chicken broth

Instructions

1. Put the small saucepan on high heat and add water. Covering the pot and letting the water soak in, the quinoa will be ready in about 15 minutes.
2. Add the oil to a large saucepan and heat it over medium-high heat while the quinoa cooks. Add the onion and cook it until it's clear and soft. It's time to boil the peas and chicken broth. Lower the heat and leave the lid off for about 5 minutes or until the peas are warm all the way through.
3. You can use either a regular or immersion blender to get the soup to the right consistency. When you add the quinoa, salt, and pepper, mix the soup that has been blended into the pan. Put everything in the oven and heat it.
4. For extra flavor, serve with extra toppings. Keep soup in a container in the fridge that won't let air in.

31. BRUSSELS SPROUTS SOUP WITH CARAMELIZED ONIONS

Prep Time: 15 Minutes | Cook Time: 55 Minutes | Total Time: 1 Hour 10 Minutes | Serving: 4

Ingredients

- 1 tbsp olive oil
- 1 pound Brussels sprouts
- 3 onions
- 1 tbsp sugar
- 4 dashes of hot pepper sauce
- ½ cup of sour cream
- 1 tsp fresh thyme
- salt and ground black pepper
- 4 cups of chicken stock

Instructions

1. In a pot over low heat, mix the onions and oil. Wrap it up and cook for 30 to 40 minutes or until it's very soft and tender. Take off the cover and sprinkle sugar on top of the onions. Leave the lid off and cook for 10 to 15 minutes until the onions are light brown. Add the Brussels sprouts and thyme to the pot and mix them in. Put the stock and salt and pepper to taste. Set the heat lower and cook for 10 minutes or until the sprouts are barely soft.
2. Let the soup cool down a bit. Use an immersion blender to blend until the mixture is smooth. Warm it up slowly again for about two minutes, and if you need to, change the seasoning.

32. CARROT GINGER LENTIL SOUP

Prep Time: 5 Minutes | Cook Time: 20 Minutes

Total Time: 25 Minutes | Serving: 4

Ingredients

- 500g carrots
- 1/2 cup of raw cashews
- 1 tsp ground turmeric
- 6 cups of vegetable stock
- 1 brown onion
- Salt
- 1 tbsp extra virgin olive oil
- Coconut cream
- 1 cup of red lentils
- 2 tsp curry powder
- 6 slices fresh ginger
- 4 cloves garlic

Instructions

1. In a pot, heat the olive oil over medium-high heat. Put in the garlic, onion, and carrots. If you want a little caramelization, cook for 4 to 5 minutes.
2. Salt, ginger, cumin, and turmeric should be added. For about one to two minutes, stir the aromatics and let them toast a bit. It should smell really good. But don't let the garlic get too hot.
3. Put in the lentils that have been rinsed, the cashews, and the vegetable stock. Slower the heat, cover, and let it simmer for 15 minutes. It should be easy to pierce with a fork when carrots are done.
4. You can use an immersion blender to blend the soup in the pot or move it to a high-speed blender and blend it until it's smooth. You should blend in parts if you have a high-speed blender. Improve the taste of the spices.
5. You can serve it in bowls with toasted bread, fresh coriander, chopped cashews, and a drizzle of coconut cream.

33. PUMPKIN RED LENTIL SOUP

Prep Time: 10 Minutes | Cook Time: 40 Minutes

Total Time: 50 Minutes | Serving: 5

Ingredients

- 1 cup of canned full-fat coconut milk
- 1-quart lower-sodium vegetable broth
- 1/2 cup of finely chopped carrots
- 1 cup of red lentils
- 3 Tbsp. extra-virgin olive oil
- 1 tsp. freshly grated ginger
- 3 Tbsp. Thai Red Curry Paste
- Juice of 1/2 lime
- 2 garlic cloves
- 1 yellow onion
- 1 cup of water
- 1/4 tsp. pumpkin pie spice
- 1 tsp. kosher salt
- 1 can pumpkin puree

Instructions

1. Heat a Dutch oven and put the oil. Put in the carrots and onion, and cook for 8 minutes. This will make it soft. Add garlic, ginger, Thai Red Curry Paste, and pumpkin pie spice. Mix them all together. One more minute of cooking will make the food smell good.
2. Put the pumpkin puree, broth, salt, and 1 cup of water. It should slowly boil. Then, put a lid on top and lower the heat to medium-low. About 30 minutes should pass before the lentils are soft. Add the coconut milk and mix well.
3. Pure half the soup in a regular blender, an immersion blender, or a food processor. Then, add the pureed half back to the pot. The soup should have some chunks in it. Add lime juice and mix it in. Serve with any toppings you like.

34. ASPARAGUS SOUP WITH LEMON AND PARMESAN

Prep Time: 15 Minutes | Cook Time: 20 Minutes

Total Time: 35 Minutes | Serving: 5

Ingredients

- ➤ 6 cups of low-sodium chicken broth
- ➤ Handful fresh herbs
- ➤ 2 tbsp freshly squeezed lemon juice
- ➤ 3 cloves garlic
- ➤ 2 bunches asparagus
- ➤ Salt
- ➤ 3 tbsp unsalted butter
- ➤ Freshly ground black pepper
- ➤ ½ cup of shredded Parmigiano-Reggiano
- ➤ 2 medium yellow onions

Instructions

1. In a big pot over medium heat, melt the butter. Add the garlic and onions, and stir them around a lot. Cook for about 8 minutes or until the onions are soft and clear. Don't let it brown; if you need to, lower the heat.
2. While you wait, cut the ends off one bunch of asparagus and set them aside. Take the rest of the spears and the other bunch of asparagus and cut them into ½-inch pieces.
3. Add the chopped asparagus, chicken broth, 1 tsp of salt, and ¼ tsp of pepper. Cover it and turn down the heat when it starts to boil. Turn down the heat and cook the veggies for 30 minutes or until they are very soft.
4. Warm up a small pot of salted water while that is going on. The asparagus tips you saved should be cooked for a few minutes or until soft but crisp. Drain the tips and put them in ice water to "shock" them. The bright green color stays the same after this. Once they are cool, drain the tips and set them aside.
5. Wet a stick blender and blend the soup until it is completely smooth. Bring the soup back to low heat and put the Parmigiano-Reggiano and lemon juice. Check the seasoning and make changes if needed. Let the soup simmer without covering it for as long as you want to make it thicker.
6. Put some soup in each bowl, and then add asparagus tips, Parmigiano-Reggiano, herbs, and freshly ground black pepper.
7. Friendly to freezers. How to do it: The soup can be frozen for up to three months. Let the soup thaw in the fridge for 12 hours, and then heat it on medium-low heat on the stove.

35. TOMATO AND ROASTED RED PEPPER SOUP

Prep Time: 10 Minutes | Cook Time: 20 Minutes

Total Time: 30 Minutes | Serving: 4

Ingredients

- 1 jar roasted red peppers
- 4 garlic cloves
- 1 cup of lower-sodium vegetable
- 1/2 tsp. cracked black pepper
- 1 medium yellow onion
- 1 can crushed tomatoes
- 3/4 tsp. salt
- 1/2 cup of Heavy Cream
- 1/3 cup of grated Parmesan cheese
- 2 Tbsp. Extra-virgin olive oil

Instructions

1. Put olive oil to a large stock pot or Dutch oven on medium heat. It will take about 8 minutes of cooking after you add the onion until it is soft. Add the garlic and cook for one more minute.
2. Put crushed tomatoes and roasted red peppers in the broth. Simmer for a while.
3. Let it cook on medium-low heat for about 15 minutes or until it gets thinner. Lower the heat after adding salt and black pepper.
4. Soup can be made smooth with an immersion blender or a hand blender. Mix in the heavy Cream and Parmesan. Check the seasonings and make any necessary changes.
5. Put the soup into bowls and top with extra black pepper and other toppings you like.

36. ROASTED PARSNIP AND PEAR SOUP

Prep Time: 10 Minutes | Cook Time: 45 Minutes

Total Time: 55 Minutes | Serving: 4

Ingredients

- ½ tsp sea salt
- 2 Bartlett pears
- 2 leeks
- 1 bay leaf
- 5 parsnips
- 4 cups of vegetable stock
- Ground black pepper
- 10 to 15 sprigs of fresh thyme
- 3 tbsp olive oil

Instructions

1. It should be 400 degrees F in the oven. Put parchment paper on the bottom of the baking sheet. Put the parsnips on the baking sheet and drizzle olive oil over them. Add sea salt & black pepper to make it taste better. Put them in the oven and toast them for 15 to 20 minutes or until they get soft and brown.
2. Put two tbsp of olive oil in a Dutch oven or soup pot and heat it over medium-low heat. After adding the leeks, cook for two to three minutes or until they smell good. After adding the pears and ½ tsp of salt, let it cook for a little longer. Then, add the roasted parsnips, bay leaf, thyme sprigs, and vegetable stock. Set a lid on top and let it cook slowly for 15 to 20 minutes.
3. Remove the bay leaf and thyme sprigs by turning off the heat and opening the pot. If you have one, there is a way to blend the soup in the pot. Carefully put the soup into an upright blender if you are using one. Don't put all the food in it, and leave the lid open so the steam can escape. Remove the lid and cover the blender with a dish towel if necessary. Mix until it's smooth. Be very careful as you blend. The mixture is going to be very hot!
4. Add fresh thyme and homemade croutons on top and serve right away.

37. ZUCCHINI BASIL SOUP

Prep Time: 15 Minutes | Cook Time: 30 Minutes

Total Time: 45 Minutes | Serving: 4

Ingredients

- 2 Zucchinis
- 1 tbsp Nutritional Yeast
- 1 Handful of Fresh Basil Leaves
- 1/2 tsp Garlic Powder
- 1 tsp Oregano
- 1 Yellow Onion
- 3 cups of Vegetable Broth
- 1/2 Avocado
- 3 Garlic Cloves
- Salt and Pepper

Instructions

1. In a big pot, cook the onion and garlic for 5-7 minutes over medium heat. So they don't stick, splash them with water.
2. Another three minutes will go by after you add the zucchini.
3. Then, add nutritional yeast, garlic powder, oregano, and vegetable broth to the pot. Mix everything.
4. Bring up the temperature. Set the pot on low heat and cover it with a lid. Let it cook for 20 minutes.
5. Mix the avocado and basil leaves into the soup after cooking.
6. Put the soup into a blender and blend it in if you have one. For a regular blender, wait a few minutes for the soup to cool down before adding it. Mix it until it's creamy and smooth.
7. If you want to change some of the seasonings, taste the soup. Bring it back to a boil, if needed, and then serve.

38. MOROCCAN CHICKPEA TOMATO STEW

Prep Time: 10 Minutes | Cook Time: 30 Minutes

Total Time: 40 Minutes | Serving: 4

Ingredients

- 1/2 tsp crushed red pepper flakes
- 2 tsp red wine vinegar
- 1 tbsp tahini
- freshly chopped parsley leaves for serving
- 1/4 tsp cinnamon
- 3 cups of cooked chickpeas
- cooked couscous for serving
- 1-2 tbsp sugar

- 1/4 tsp ground cloves
- 1 tsp ground coriander
- 1 tsp ground cumin
- 3/4 tsp kosher salt
- 2 cups of low-sodium vegetable broth
- 1 tbsp Olive Oil
- 2 pounds chopped plum tomatoes
- 1 white or yellow onion
- 4 cloves garlic

Instructions

1. In a big pot over medium-low heat, warm the olive oil. Add the onion when the oil starts to shimmer. Twice a minute, or until the onion is soft and clear, stir it while it's cooking. Add the garlic and stir it in a few times. If it starts to stick, add a tbsp or two of water. Leave it to cook for two more minutes.

2. Put the tomatoes in the pot. To ensure the whole peeled tomatoes in the can are well crushed, use a potato masher or the back of a large spoon. It should have coriander, cumin, red pepper flakes, cloves, and cinnamon. Add 1 tbsp of sugar and salt. Stir the tomatoes around a lot as you cook them for 10 minutes or until they get thicker and bubbly. Turn down the heat to a simmer, add the broth or water, and cook for another 10 minutes with the lid off.

3. Add the tahini and blend part of the soup with an immersion blender so you can still see some tomato chunks, but the mixture is thick and looks like a chunky soup.

4. The chickpeas and vinegar should be mixed in. Bring it to a boil again. If you want, you can taste the stew and change the seasonings. If you want, you can serve it with your choice of grain and a sprinkle of parsley.

39. VEGAN LENTIL STEW

Prep Time: 10 Minutes | Cook Time: 30 Minutes | Total Time: 40 Minutes | Serving: 6

Ingredients

- 8 cups of vegetable broth
- 2 large carrots diced
- 1 pound brown lentils sorted
- 4 cloves garlic minced
- 1/4 tsp black pepper
- 4 Roma tomatoes diced
- 1 1/2 tsp kosher salt
- 1/4 cup of sofrito optional
- 2 stalks of celery diced
- 2 tbsp olive oil
- 1 cup of yellow onion diced
- 1 large bay leaf
- 1 1/2 tbsp Garam Masala Spice Blend
- 3/4 cup of green bell pepper diced
- 1/4 cup of tamari

Instructions

1. In a 4 1/2-quart Dutch oven, heat the olive oil to a medium-high level.
2. After the oil in the pot shatters, add the bell pepper, garlic, onion, and carrots.
3. For three to four minutes, or until they look shiny and turn opaque, saute the vegetables.
4. Mix the sofrito into the cooking vegetables in the pot, then let it cook for one more minute.
5. Include the Garam Masala Spice Blend and chopped tomatoes in the pot. In the pot, cook the tomatoes for 6 minutes or until they have given up most of their liquid.
6. Include the lentils that have been rinsed and the tamari in the pot.
7. After mixing the lentils with the other ingredients in the pot, put the vegetable broth and stir it all together. Put the bay leaf in the mix and mix everything.
8. Bring the liquid's temperature up. Lower the heat and cover the pot when the liquid starts to boil.
9. Low heat for 25 minutes will make the lentils soft. Five minutes later, make sure the lentils are still not boiling.
10. To keep the heavier ingredients from sticking to the bottom of the pot, mix the stew every 10 minutes as it cooks.
11. Eliminate the heat. Take the bay leaf and 2 cups of lentils out of the pot and throw them away.
12. Use an immersion blender to make the lentils a little smoother. It's fine to have smaller pieces of vegetables and whole lentils.
13. Optional: carefully move small amounts of the stew to your blender at a time. Remove the plastic plug from the middle to let air into the blender lid. Use a folded towel to cover the lid's hole to keep water out. Make the stew mostly smooth by pureeing it for 30 seconds. After the stew is smooth, add the lentils you set aside back to the pot and mix everything.
14. To reheat the stew, set the stove to warm. Put the stew into bowls, top with avocado slices and diced onion to serve.

40. SMOKEY BLACK BEAN SOUP

Prep Time: 10 Minutes | Cook Time: 15 Minutes

Total Time: 25 Minutes | Serving: 6

Ingredients

- ➢ 1 can diced tomatoes
- ➢ 1 tsp smoked paprika
- ➢ 1 sweet onion chopped
- ➢ 2 tbsp avocado oil
- ➢ 3 garlic cloves crushed
- ➢ 3 cans of black beans drained
- ➢ 1 red bell pepper chopped
- ➢ 1 lime juiced
- ➢ 1/2 tsp ground cumin
- ➢ 2 tbsp adobo sauce
- ➢ 2 cups of vegetable broth

Instructions

1. Put the onion, red bell pepper, and oil in a large soup pot. For 5 to 7 minutes, or until golden brown, cook over medium heat.
2. Then add the black beans, adobo sauce, cumin, salt, and pepper. Stir in the garlic and the vegetable broth.
3. When the soup starts to boil, put the lid on the pot and let it cook for 10 to 15 minutes.
4. Either use an immersion blender or a high-speed blender to pulse the soup until it's smooth but still has some chunks in it.
5. Include the fresh lime juice. Garnish with avocado, tortilla chips, cilantro, green onions, sour Cream, or Greek yogurt, and serve.

41. COMFORTING PEA & HAM SOUP

Prep Time: 10 Minutes | Cook Time: 3 Minutes

Total Time: 13 Minutes | Serving: 4

Ingredients

- ➢ 2 carrots
- ➢ 2 cloves garlic
- ➢ 1 onion
- ➢ 1 bay leaf
- ➢ Salt and pepper

- ➢ 1 ham hock
- ➢ 1 cup of frozen baby peas
- ➢ 2L water
- ➢ 2 celery stalks
- ➢ 500g green split peas

Chorizo & bread croutons:

- ➢ 1 chorizo sausage
- ➢ 1 tbsp olive oil

- ➢ 4-6 slices of bread
- ➢ Salt and pepper

Instructions

1. Put the ham hock in a large pot and add 2L of water to cover it. Bring to a boil over high heat. Then lower the heat to low and let it cook for an hour and a half to two hours, or until the ham is soft and falling off the bone. Take the ham hock out of the pot and set it somewhere to cool down. Take the meat off the bone and shred it into small pieces once it's cool.
2. Put in the bay leaf, onion, garlic, carrot, celery, frozen baby peas, and bay leaf. Simmer for 10 to 15 minutes or until the vegetables are soft. Put in the split peas and cook for another 30 to 45 minutes, until the peas are soft and cooked.
3. To smooth the soup, take out the bay leaf and use an immersion blender or put the soup in a blender. You can also leave some chunky pieces if you'd rather. Mix the shredded ham into the pot after adding it. Add pepper and salt to taste.
4. Serve hot with toast or crusty bread. You can add croutons, chopped fresh herbs like parsley or thyme, sour Cream, or plain Greek yogurt as a topping.

Chorizo & bread croutons:

1. Medium-high heat should be used for the big pan. Put olive oil in the pan. To cook the chorizo slices, heat the pan and add the slices. Cook for two to three minutes on each side until nice and brown. Take the chorizo out of the pan and put it on a plate.
2. Put the bread cubes in the same pan as the chorizo fat and toss them around until they are all covered. Over medium heat, stir the bread cubes now and then until they are golden brown and crispy, which should take about 5 to 7 minutes.
3. Put the chorizo slices back in the pan to heat through after the bread cubes are done. Put it on top of the soup.

42. BUTTERNUT SQUASH HUMMUS

Prep Time: 10 Minutes | Cook Time: 30 Minutes

Total Time: 40 Minutes | Serving: 6

Ingredients

- Sesame seeds
- 1-2 cloves garlic
- Juice of 4-5 lemons
- Zest of 1 lemon
- ⅓ cup of olive oil
- 3-4 Tbsp tahini
- Salt and pepper
- 2 cups of roasted butternut squash
- 2 cups of dried chickpeas

Instructions

1. Fill chickpeas with water: Use a medium-sized saucepan and add chickpeas. Add a little over an inch of water and cover them. After 5 minutes, turn off the heat and let it sit for an hour. After that, drain the water and put the chickpeas back in the pot.
2. For chickpeas, cook: Add two to three inches of water to the cover. First, bring it to a boil. Then lower the heat and let it simmer for 3–4 hours with the lid open.
3. Remove the skin from the squash while it's cooking and cut it into small pieces. Taste and put more salt and pepper if needed. At 350°, bake it for 30 to 60 minutes, flipping it over every 30 minutes.
4. Mix and taste: Put everything into a blender and blend until the mixture is smooth. You can add sesame seeds, pumpkin seeds, and olive oil as a garnish. Keep in the fridge for up to a week.

43. WHIPPED CREAM

Prep Time: 5 Minutes | Cook Time: 5 Minutes

Total Time: 10 Minutes | Serving: 6

Ingredients

- 2 cups of heavy Cream
- 2 tbsp powdered sugar

Instructions

1. Put sugar that has been ground into heavy Cream in a large bowl.
2. With a stick blender, pulse the Cream and sugar together on and off until stiff peaks form.
3. You can serve it right away or put it in the fridge for about three hours.

44. PISTACHIO CREAM

Prep Time: 5 Minutes | Cook Time: 00 Minutes

Total Time: 5 Minutes | Serving: 6

Ingredients

- 4 1/2 ounces homemade pistachio paste
- 12 ounces heavy Cream

Instructions

1. Put the pistachio paste and Cream into a measuring cup, jar, or container that is just big enough for the immersion blender's head. The cream layer must be deeper to blend if the jar is too big. The blades won't be able to reach the paste at the bottom if the jar is too small. The food could also be put in the bowl of a food processor.
2. After processing the ingredients, the mixture should be smooth and thick, like frosting. Carefully examine the Cream's feel and structure to discover the optimal time for your machine. Immediately spread it on the cake, ice cream, or fresh fruit tarts, store it in a container that won't let air in, and chill it for up to a week.

45. MAYONNAISE

Prep Time: 5 Minutes | Cook Time: 00 Minutes

Total Time: 5 Minutes | Serving: 12

Ingredients

- ½ tbsp lemon juice
- 1 cup of avocado oil
- ¼ tsp Dijon mustard
- 1 tsp white wine vinegar
- ¼ tsp sea salt
- 1 whole egg

Instructions

1. Put the egg, vinegar, mustard, lemon juice, and salt in the jar that came with your immersion blender. Pour the oil on top slowly, and wait a minute for it to settle.
2. Put the egg yolk in the jar and press down hard. Then, cover it with the stick blender. Put it on and hold it against the bottom of the jar for ten to fifteen seconds. Do not move it.
3. Along with the mayonnaise thins and thickens, slowly move the stick blender up and down to mix the ingredients all the way through.
4. Mix the mayonnaise, put it in a container without air, and put it in the fridge.

46. CHICKPEA CHOCOLATE SPREAD

Prep Time: 5 Minutes | Cook Time: 00 Minutes

Total Time: 5 Minutes | Serving: 10

Ingredients

- ¼ tsp salt
- 3 tbsp olive oil
- 4 tbsp honey
- 4 tbsp cocoa powder
- 400 g chickpeas rinsed
- 50 ml water

Instructions

1. Put the honey, olive oil, and water in the blender. Add the cocoa, salt, and drained chickpeas.
2. Blend until smooth. If you need to, scrape down the blender a few times. You may need to add more water to get the right consistency. Be careful not to add too much at once!

47. WHIPPED RICOTTA CHEESE SPREAD

Prep Time: 5 Minutes | Cook Time: 00 Minutes

Total Time: 5 Minutes | Serving: 12

Ingredients

- 16-24 ounces of full fat ricotta cheese
- 2 tbsp extra virgin olive oil

Instructions

1. Mix the ricotta cheese and oil in a food processor bowl with a blade.
2. Whip for about one to two minutes or until smooth and creamy.
3. Put the oil and ricotta cheese in a bowl.
4. To make it smooth and creamy, mix quickly with an immersion blender. Clean off the sides, and do it again if you need to.

To Serve:

1. Spread the whipped cheese evenly in a bowl or platter that is not too deep. Add any toppings you like, and serve with slices of crusty baguette.

48. BEETROOT HUMMUS

Prep Time: 20 Minutes | Cook Time: 00 Minutes

Total Time: 20 Minutes | Serving: 4

Ingredients

- 2 tbsp of tahini
- 1/2 lemon juice
- 2 cups of boiled chickpeas
- Salt
- 1/2 tsp of cumin
- 2 small beets
- 2 cloves of garlic
- 1/4 cup of olive oil

Instructions

1. Put the peeled beets in a saucepan with enough water to cover them. Bring to a boil with the lid on. Once it's done, drain the water and let the beets cool.
2. Beets, chickpeas, tahini, lemon juice, olive oil, cumin, garlic, and salt that have been boiled should all be put in a large bowl. Use an immersion blender to blend the ingredients until the mixture is smooth.
3. Put the mix in the bowl for serving.

49. SUN-DRIED TOMATO SPREAD

Prep Time: 5 Minutes | Cook Time: 00 Minutes

Total Time: 5 Minutes | Serving: 11

Ingredients

- 1 tsp. garlic powder
- 1 tsp. dried basil
- 1 8.5- ounce. Jar sun-dried tomatoes
- ½ tsp. kosher salt
- 1 tbsp brown sugar
- 1 6- ounce. can tomato paste

Instructions

1. Combine the ingredients and blend with a food processor or immersion blender until the texture is "smoothly chunky." Now it's over! Refrigerate for up to a week. Place on wraps and sandwiches, mix into pasta and roasted vegetables, or mix into cream cheese to make a great dip for wheat crackers.

50. LEMON AND DILL HUMMUS

Prep Time: 10 Minutes | Cook Time: 00 Minutes

Total Time: 10 Minutes | Serving: 6

Ingredients

- 2 tbsp Sour Cream
- 2 tbsp fresh Dill
- 1/4 tsp Paprika
- pinch of Cayenne Pepper
- 1/4 cup of Avocado Oil
- 3 tbsp Lemon Juice
- 1/4 tsp Sea Salt
- 1 1/4 cups of canned cooked Chickpeas
- 1/2 tsp Cumin

Instructions

1. Put everything in a mason jar with a wide mouth.
2. Blend until smooth with an immersion blender.
3. Add tortilla chips and vegetables to the dish. It can be kept in the fridge for up to a week.

51. ROASTED GARLIC BUTTER

Prep Time: 5 Minutes | Cook Time: 20 Minutes

Total Time: 25 Minutes | Serving: 8

Ingredients

- ¼ cup of air fryer roasted garlic
- 1/2 tsp cracked black pepper
- 1 tsp finely minced fresh rosemary
- ½ cup of salted butter

Instructions

1. Mix butter, pepper, rosemary, and roasted garlic.
2. Mix until well combined.
3. Store in the fridge until needed.

52. BLACK BEAN DIP

Prep Time: 20 Minutes | Cook Time: 00 Minutes

Total Time: 20 Minutes | Serving: 10

Ingredients

- 2 cans black beans
- 1/2 cup of crumbled queso fresco
- 1/2 cup of sour cream
- 1/2 tsp. chili powder
- 4 ounce. cream cheese
- Juice of 1/2 lime

- 1 cup of shredded pepper jack
- 2 cloves garlic
- 1 jalapeno
- 1/2 tsp. ground cumin
- 1/2 cup of shredded cheddar

For Garnish:

- Tortilla chips
- 1 cup of cherry tomatoes
- 1/2 red onion

- Freshly chopped cilantro
- 1 jalapeno
- 1/4 cup of crumbled queso fresco

Instructions

1. Add beans, sour cream, cream cheese, Jalapeno, garlic, cumin, chili powder, lime juice, and queso fresco to a 6-quart Instant Pot. Add pepper and salt for seasoning. Put the Instant Pot's lid on and select Pressure. Simmer for ten minutes on high.
2. As directed by the manufacturer, quickly release and remove the lid. Make sure the beans are smooth by blending them with an immersion blender.
3. If desired, move the dip to a medium skillet that is safe for the oven, top with pepper jack and cheddar, and bake for 15 minutes at 350° until the cheese is melted.
4. Add tomatoes, red onion, cilantro, queso fresco, and Jalapeno slices as garnish. Warm up and serve with chips.

53. WHIPPED SWEET POTATOES

Prep Time: 10 Minutes | Cook Time: 25 Minutes

Total Time: 35 Minutes | Serving: 6

Ingredients

- ➤ 1/2 tsp pepper
- ➤ 1/2 tsp sea salt
- ➤ 2 tbsp butter
- ➤ pinch of nutmeg
- ➤ 1/4 cup of heavy cream
- ➤ 4 large sweet potatoes
- ➤ 1 tsp vanilla extract

Instructions

1. Cut sweet potatoes into large pieces. After adding them to a large pot of cold water, bring it to a boil. Lower the heat to medium-high after the water reaches a boiling point. Cook until the sweet potatoes are fork-tender, another 20 to 30 minutes.
2. After draining the water, put the potatoes back in the pot. Add butter, heavy cream, nutmeg, vanilla, salt, and pepper. To beat the mixture, use a food processor, stand mixer, hand mixer, immersion blender, masher, or fork.
3. Present and enjoy!

54. CREAMY AVOCADO SAUCE

Prep Time: 5 Minutes | Cook Time: 00 Minutes

Total Time: 5 Minutes | Serving: 4

Ingredients

- salt and pepper
- 1 avocado
- 1 tbsp lime juice
- ½ large fresh jalapeno
- ½ cup of plain Greek yogurt

Instructions

1. Place the yogurt, lime juice, and salt and pepper in a small food processor or mixer. Add the avocado after peeling it. Cut the Jalapeno half into about three smaller pieces to make blending easier.
2. Blend until very smooth, about one or two minutes. As you please, serve. Refrigerate after covering.

55. ROMA TOMATO SAUCE

Prep Time: 5 Minutes | Cook Time: 20 Minutes

Total Time: 25 Minutes | Serving: 6

Ingredients

- 1/2 tsp pepper
- 5 pounds tomatoes
- 1 clove garlic minced
- 1/4 cup of olive oil
- 1/2 tsp salt

Instructions

1. Put the tomatoes in a big pot. Stir in the salt and pepper. Place tomatoes on medium-high heat and bring to a boil. Boil for twenty minutes. More liquid will form as the tomatoes begin to break down.
2. Mix in the olive oil and the garlic. Run the immersion blender on low until the desired consistency of sauce is achieved.
3. Serve right away or put in the fridge to use within a few days.
4. As an alternative, you could freeze them in freezer bags for use in upcoming months.

56. HOLLANDAISE SAUCE

Prep Time: 5 Minutes | Cook Time: 5 Minutes

Total Time: 10 Minutes | Serving: 4

Ingredients

- ➤ 1 stick unsalted butter
- ➤ 1 tsp water
- ➤ Pinch cayenne pepper
- ➤ 1 tsp lemon juice
- ➤ Kosher salt
- ➤ 2 large egg yolks

Instructions

1. In a cup of just large enough to hold the head of an immersion blender, whisk together the egg yolks, water, lemon juice, and a pinch of salt. Heat a small saucepan over high heat and melt butter, stirring constantly until foaming stops. Put butter into a liquid measuring cup of that holds one cup.

2. Switch on the immersion blender by inserting its head into the bottom of the cup. Pour hot butter into a measuring cup of slowly in a thin stream while the blender runs continuously. With the egg yolk and lemon juice, it ought to emulsify. To aid in emulsification, tilt the blender head slightly if necessary. Pour until all of the butter has been added. The consistency of the sauce should be such that it coats a spoon without becoming too runny. To thin it out to the right consistency, if it's too thick, whisk in a tiny amount of warm water, one tbsp at a time. Put a dash of hot sauce or cayenne pepper and season to taste. Transfer to a small pot with a lid and keep warm for up to one hour before serving, or serve immediately. It is not possible to chill and reheat hollandaise.

57. SWEET & TANGY BBQ SAUCE

Prep Time: 20 Minutes | Cook Time: 10 Minutes

Total Time: 30 Minutes | Serving: 2

Ingredients

- A few dashes hot sauce
- 1 clove garlic
- 1/2 tbsp olive oil
- 1 tbsp tomato paste
- 1 tsp liquid smoke
- 1/4 medium red onion
- 1/2 tsp cumin
- 2 tbsp packed brown sugar
- 1 tbsp molasses
- 1 tsp salt
- Freshly ground pepper
- 1 tsp Dijon or brown mustard
- 1 can tomato puree
- 2 tsp Worcestershire sauce
- 1 tbsp cider vinegar

Instructions

1. Warm up a small amount of olive oil in a medium-sized saucepan over medium heat. Put the onions and cook for about five minutes or until soft. Put the garlic and cook for a minute or two more.
2. Turn the heat low and stir in the cumin and tomato paste. Add the remaining ingredients, including the tomato puree. Once mixed, simmer for five to ten minutes or until the desired thickness is achieved. As you taste, adjust the salt, pepper, or other seasonings.
3. Pour the sauce into an immersion blender and process it until it becomes smooth. If you like a thinner sauce, add a tbsp or two more water at a time.
4. You can freeze this sauce for up to three months or keep it in the refrigerator for about two weeks.

58. AVOCADO DIP

Prep Time: 5 Minutes | Cook Time: 00 Minutes

Total Time: 5 Minutes | Serving: 6

Ingredients

- ➢ 1 Jalapeno
- ➢ 1 juicy lime
- ➢ 1 large avocado
- ➢ 1/2-1 tsp sea salt
- ➢ 1-2 Tbsp water
- ➢ 1 cup of cilantro

Instructions

1. Add cilantro, lime juice, sea salt, 1 Tbsp water, and a deseeded Jalapeno in a jar that fits your immersion blender. Blend until fully liquid. Add extra water as necessary.
2. Cut the avocado in half, remove the pit, then add the flesh to the cilantro water. Process until smooth and serve.

59. BEARNAISE SAUCE

Prep Time: 10 Minutes | Cook Time: 2 Minutes

Total Time: 12 Minutes | Serving: 4

Ingredients

Infused Vinegar :

- 1 1/2 tbsp white wine
- 1/4 tsp black pepper
- 2 sprigs tarragon
- 1 1/2 tbsp white wine vinegar
- 1 eschalot

Bearnaise Sauce:

- 1/2 tbsp tarragon leaves
- 1/2 tbsp chervil
- 3 egg yolks
- 1/4 tsp salt
- 16 tbsp unsalted butter

Instructions

1. Mix the ingredients for the Infused Vinegar in a small saucepan over medium-low heat.
2. After two minutes of simmering, remove from heat and leave to infuse for five minutes.
3. Press through the strainer to extract as much liquid as you can. About 1 tbsp of liquid should be consumed. Allow to cool for five minutes before using.
4. Melt the butter in a jug by heating it in the microwave.
5. Let it stand for 30 seconds until the clarified butter sits on top of the milky whites that have settled to the bottom.
6. Remove 175g, or 3/4 cup the clarified butter and throw away the leftover milky whites. While hot, use it in this recipe.
7. Put the egg yolks, salt, and vinegar in a tall, narrow container that can accommodate the blender stick to the bottom. Blitz for a little while to blend.
8. Put the stick blender on high and gradually pour in the butter over about a minute.
9. Once all of the butter has been added, blitz for an additional 10 seconds while raising and lowering the stick.
10. Blend in 1 tbsp of water after adding it. When the Bearnaise Sauce is thick enough to oouncee over a steak and coat it thickly, add extra water, one tsp at a time.
11. Add chervil and tarragon and stir.
12. Utilize right away or hold warm until needed. I use a thermos; a decent one will maintain the temperature for at least an hour. Store at room temperature or warm. For reheating and storing.

60. CILANTRO LIME SAUCE

Prep Time: 5 Minutes | Cook Time: 00 Minutes

Total Time: 5 Minutes | Serving: 6

Ingredients

- 1 cup of cilantro
- 1 clove garlic
- 1/2 tsp pepper
- 1–2 limes
- 1/2 cup of greek yogurt
- 1/2 tsp salt
- 2 tbsp avocado
- Optional: 1 jalapeno

Instructions

1. Mix the ingredients. Mix all ingredients in a big bowl or blender.
2. Mix. Process until a smooth sauce forms, either with an immersion blender. Savor it as a marinade, dressing, or dipping sauce!

61. WHIPPED FETA DIP

Prep Time: 10 Minutes | Cook Time: 00 Minutes

Total Time: 10 Minutes | Serving: 4

Ingredients

- 3 tbsp olive oil
- 10 ounce. block feta cheese
- 2 tbsp pistachios
- 1 Persian cucumber
- 8 ounce. plain Greek yogurt
- juice and zest of 1/2 a lemon
- 1 tbsp fresh dill
- Naan bread cut into triangles
- 1/4 tsp garlic powder
- salt and pepper
- 1/3 cup of cherry tomatoes

Instructions

1. Feta, Greek yogurt, lemon zest, olive oil, garlic powder, salt, and pepper should all be combined in a big bowl. Using an immersion blender, blend until fully blended and creamy. It ought to require several minutes.
2. Spoon the feta whipped onto a small plate or into a shallow bowl.
3. Add pistachios, tomatoes, cucumbers, and dill on top.
4. Accompany the dish right away with pita or naan chips and lemon wedges.

62. ROASTED RED PEPPER DIP

Prep Time: 20 Minutes | Cook Time: 15 Minutes | Total Time: 35 Minutes | Serving: 6

Ingredients

- salt
- 5 cloves garlic
- 1 yellow pepper
- 3 red peppers
- Gefen Olive Oil
- pepper

Instructions

1. Turn the oven on to broil.
2. Place every pepper on a baking sheet covered with Gefen Parchment Paper, cut side down. Give it a liberal drizzle of olive oil. After placing in the oven, broil the peppers for 15 minutes until they are mostly charred or blackened. After adding the garlic cloves, broil for an additional four minutes.
3. Take it out of the oven and allow it to cool slightly. Slice the peppers. Put the garlic and peppers in a medium-sized bowl. Pour in any liquid that has been collected in the pan. Blend everything with an immersion blender until the right consistency is achieved. Season with salt and pepper to taste.

63. BLUEBERRY CHIPOTLE BBQ SAUCE

Prep Time: 10 Minutes | Cook Time: 30 Minutes | Total Time: 40 Minutes | Serving: 2

Ingredients

- 1 tbsp Worcestershire sauce
- 2 tbsp honey
- 1/2 tsp black pepper
- 1 small onion finely chopped
- 1/4 tsp cayenne pepper
- 1/4 cup of brown sugar
- 1 cup of fresh frozen blueberries
- 1 tsp smoked paprika
- 1/2 tbsp ground cinnamon
- 2 cloves garlic minced
- 1 tsp ground cumin
- 1 tbsp adobo sauce
- 2 chipotle peppers in adobo sauce
- 1/4 cup of apple cider vinegar
- 1 cup of ketchup
- 1/2 tsp salt
- 1 tbsp olive oil

Instructions

1. To begin, place a medium saucepan over medium heat with the olive oil. Add the finely chopped onion and cook for about 5 minutes or until it becomes transparent. Cook the minced garlic for one to two minutes or until it becomes fragrant.
2. Add the adobo sauce and the chopped chipotle peppers. Add the frozen or fresh blueberries and cook for 3–4 minutes to allow them to soften and release their juices.
3. Add the honey, Worcestershire sauce, apple cider vinegar, and ketchup. Toss to mix in all the ingredients thoroughly.

4. If you like extra spicy food, add the cayenne pepper, ground cumin, ground cinnamon, brown sugar, smoked paprika, and salt. Mix everything thoroughly to incorporate the sauce fully.

5. Heat the mixture until it simmers gently. After lowering the heat to low, simmer it for 20-25 minutes, stirring now and then. The flavors will combine, and the sauce should become thicker.

64. LEMON HERB TAHINI SAUCE

Prep Time: 15 Minutes | Cook Time: 00 Minutes

Total Time: 15 Minutes | Serving: 2

Ingredients

- 4 Tbsp Water
- 1/4 tsp of Black Pepper
- 1 tsp of Salt
- 2 tsp of Fresh Thyme
- Zest juice of 1 Lemon
- 1 Tbsp of Fresh Parsley
- 1/4 cup of Olive Oil
- 3 Tbsp of Tahini Paste
- 2 Tbsp of Honey
- 1 tsp of Dijon Mustard

Instructions

1. Fresh flat-leaf parsley should be chopped, and the thyme leaves should be removed from their stems.
2. After zesting the lemon, cut it in half and extract the juice.
3. Fill the cup of the immersion blender with 1/4 cup of olive oil.
4. Add the lemon juice, two tbsp of honey, and three tbsp of tahini paste to the oil.
5. Add the lemon zest, chopped parsley, 2 tsp fresh thyme, 1 tsp Dijon mustard, 1/4 tsp black pepper, one tsp salt, and a chopped tbsp of parsley.
6. With the immersion blender, begin blending the ingredients. You'll discover that it's pretty thick. One tbsp of water at a time, or until the desired consistency, is added. Savor this sauce with whatever and everything you choose!

65. SPINACH ARTICHOKE DIP

Prep Time: 10 Minutes | Cook Time: 25 Minutes

Total Time: 35 Minutes | Serving: 6

Ingredients

- ½ cup of parmesan cheese
- ½ tsp pepper
- 1 tsp salt
- 10 ounces frozen chopped spinach
- 2 tbsp minced garlic
- 12 – 14 ounces canned
- 8 ounces cream cheese
- 1 box of Wheat Thins
- 1 cup of shredded mozzarella cheese
- ½ cup of sour cream

Instructions

1. Process the artichokes, spinach, cream cheese, sour cream, garlic, pepper, and salt in a big bowl of an immersion blender until the desired consistency is reached.
2. Add mozzarella and parmesan cheese and stir.
3. After transferring the dip to an oven-safe dish, bake it at 350 degrees for everything to melt and get thoroughly heated.
4. Accompany with your preferred crackers.

66. SWEET CHILI SAUCE

Prep Time: 20 Minutes | Cook Time: 00 Minutes

Total Time: 20 Minutes | Serving: 3

Ingredients

- 5 cups of apple cider vinegar
- 4 cups of sugar
- 2 cup of red Serrano chilies
- Black pepper
- 1 cup of water
- Sea salt
- 5 cloves garlic
- 2 tsp ginger

Instructions

1. Press "start/stop," set the pressure cooker to "sear," change the time to 15 minutes, and add 1 cup of vinegar, ginger, garlic, and chilies. Simmer for about ten minutes or until the chilies are tender.
2. Puree ingredients in an immersion blender until smooth.
3. Stir in the remaining vinegar, sugar, and water. Shut the lid and lock it. Press "start/stop" after adjusting the time to 7 minutes and setting the pressure cooker to "soup." When finished, release the pressure quickly and confirm that it has wholly released before opening the lid.
4. Gently remove the lid to check the seasoning of the sauce. If necessary, add salt and pepper.

67. GREEK SALAD DRESSING

Prep Time: 10 Minutes | Cook Time: 00 Minutes

Total Time: 10 Minutes | Serving: 8

Ingredients

- ½ cup of olive oil
- 1 tsp dried oregano
- ¼ tsp salt
- ¼ tsp black pepper
- 2 medium garlic cloves crushed
- 2 tbsp lemon juice
- 3 tbsp red
- 1 tsp Dijon mustard

Instructions

1. Put everything into a mason jar with a wide mouth.
2. Using an immersion blender, blend for approximately 15 seconds or until smooth and creamy.

68. CAESAR SALAD DRESSING

Prep Time: 5 Minutes | Cook Time: 00 Minutes

Total Time: 5 Minutes | Serving: 16

Ingredients

- 1/4 cup of Parmigiano Reggiano cheese
- 1 clove garlic
- 1 1/2 tsp Dijon mustard
- 1 pasteurized egg
- 1 cup of olive oil
- 4 Tbsp fresh lemon juice
- 1/2 tsp salt
- 1/2 tsp fresh cracked black pepper
- 1 1/2 tsp anchovy paste

Instructions

1. Place every component inside a sizable mason jar. Verify that the oil and egg are both at room temperature.
2. Place an immersion blender inside the jar and activate it. Blend until the dressing has emulsified, pulling up as you go. It won't take more than a few seconds. After stirring it, taste it and adjust the seasoning. To get it just right, taste it first. You might prefer a little extra lemon or anchovies. Every time, I add extra cracked pepper.
3. Eat after two weeks and store in the refrigerator.

69. AVOCADO CILANTRO LIME DRESSING

Prep Time: 5 Minutes | Cook Time: 00 Minutes

Total Time: 5 Minutes | Serving: 14

Ingredients

- salt to taste
- juice of one lime
- 1 cup of avocado oil
- 1 small avocado
- ½ cup of cilantro
- 1 clove garlic

Instructions

1. All ingredients should be combined in a container and blended smoothly using an immersion blender.
2. Store in the fridge for up to a week in an airtight container.

70. BLUE CHEESE DRESSING

Prep Time: 5 Minutes | Cook Time: 00 Minutes

Total Time: 5 Minutes | Serving: 4

Ingredients

- 1-2 TB bacon pieces
- 1/3 cup of blue cheese crumbles
- 3 TB sour cream yogurt
- 1/2 TB lemon juice
- 2 TB mayonnaise homemade
- salt and pepper

Instructions

1. Combine the mayonnaise, lemon juice, sour cream, and crumbled blue cheese in a medium-sized bowl. Using an immersion blender, process the ingredients until the desired consistency is reached. Usually, I blend for ten to fifteen seconds. Blend the ingredients until the dressing is smooth and, if desired, add crumbled bacon.

71. RASPBERRY SALAD DRESSING

Prep Time: 5 Minutes | Cook Time: 00 Minutes

Total Time: 5 Minutes | Serving: 3

Ingredients

- ½ tsp Dijon mustard
- 1 cup of fresh raspberries
- 6 tbsp extra virgin olive oil mild
- 1-2 tbsp clear honey
- fine sea salt
- 1 tbsp apple cider vinegar

Instructions

1. Use an immersion blender to blend the raspberries. Even if you use a fork to smash them, the dressing won't be as creamy. Strain the blended raspberries to remove all the seeds using a fine-mesh sieve.
2. One cup of fresh raspberries
3. Put them back in the blender or mixing bowl with the vinegar, honey, mustard, salt, and pepper. Blend until smooth once more.
4. Mix 1 tbsp apple cider vinegar, ½ tsp Dijon mustard, and 1-2 tbsp clear honey.
5. Olive oil should be added gradually and blended until the vinaigrette emulsifies. Put a little honey, salt, and pepper to taste.
6. Six tbsp of extra virgin olive oil, fine sea salt, and freshly ground black pepper.

72. PALEO HONEY MUSTARD DRESSING

Prep Time: 5 Minutes | Cook Time: 00 Minutes

Total Time: 5 Minutes | Serving: 8

Ingredients

- 2 tbsp red wine vinegar
- 1/2 tsp sea salt
- 2 tbsp mustard
- 2 tbsp honey
- 1 tsp onion powder
- 1/2 cup of mayonnaise
- 1/4 cup of olive oil

Instructions

1. In a blender, mix all ingredients and pulse just long enough to blend fully.
2. Alternatively, you could put all the ingredients in a mason jar, blend them with an immersion blender, or just slam the lid down until the honey melts and mixes in.

73. RANCH DRESSING

Prep Time: 5 Minutes | Cook Time: 00 Minutes

Total Time: 5 Minutes | Serving: 12

Ingredients

- ¾ cup of sour cream
- ¾ cup of high-quality mayonnaise
- 1 tbsp lemon juice
- 1 garlic clove
- ¼ cup of milk
- ½ tsp salt
- 1 bunch parsley
- ½ tsp pepper
- 1 bunch chives

Instructions

1. Place all the ingredients in an immersion blender and blend.
2. To taste, add additional salt and pepper.

74. GREEK YOGURT RANCH DRESSING

Prep Time: 10 Minutes | Cook Time: Minutes

Total Time: 10 Minutes | Serving: 2

Ingredients

- 2–3 tbsp milk
- 1 cup of plain Greek Yogurt
- 1 tsp lemon juice
- 1 tsp dried dill
- 1/2 tsp onion powder
- 1/2 tsp kosher salt
- 1/2 tsp stone ground mustard
- 1 tsp dried parsley
- 1/2 tsp garlic powder

Instructions

1. Everything should be put in a medium-sized bowl and thoroughly whisked. Alternatively, as demonstrated above, add ingredients to a deep enough cup and blend with an immersion blender.
2. If you want a thinner consistency, put more milk and taste test to see if you need more salt.

75. LEMON TAHINI SALAD DRESSING

Prep Time: 5 Minutes | Cook Time: 00 Minutes

Total Time: 5 Minutes | Serving: 11

Ingredients

- 1/4 cup plus 1 tbsp water
- 1 lemon
- 2 tsp honey
- 3/4 tsp coarse kosher salt
- 1/2 cup of sesame tahini
- 1 clove garlic
- 2 tbsp extra-virgin olive oil

Instructions

1. Press the entire lemon into the cutting board and roll it on its side using the palm of your hand. Cut in half, then extract the juice. For this recipe, three tbsp are required.
2. Mince garlic cloves roughly. Add a pinch of salt and mash using the back of a knife, and pulse the mixture until a paste forms. Scrape into an immersion blender jar.
3. Stir in the honey, oil, lemon, tahini, and water. Blend until smooth.
4. To thin the dressing, add one tbsp of water and blend. Add one tbsp at a time until the desired consistency is reached.

76. AVOCADO LIME DRESSING

Prep Time: 5 Minutes | Cook Time: 00 Minutes

Total Time: 5 Minutes | Serving: 8

Ingredients

- ¼ tsp cracked black pepper
- 1 tbsp lime juice
- water
- 1 clove garlic
- ¼ tsp salt
- zest of ½ a lime
- 2 tbsp extra virgin olive oil
- 1 avocado
- ¼ cup of Greek yogurt

Instructions

1. Place all the ingredients in a tiny food processor or blender. We made use of a jug and an immersion blender.
2. Blend the dressing until it becomes creamy and smooth.
3. Although we like our dressing thick, you can adjust the consistency by adding a small amount of water. Just be careful not to thin it out too much by adding tiny amounts of water at a time.
4. Keep refrigerated for four to five days in an airtight jar. Again, you can thin out the dressing if you'd like by adding a small amount of water and mixing thoroughly. As it cools, the dressing will get even thicker

77. RASPBERRY POPPY SEED DRESSING

Prep Time: 5 Minutes | Cook Time: 00 Minutes

Total Time: 5 Minutes | Serving: 1

Ingredients
- pinch salt
- 1 Tbsp poppy seeds
- 2 Tbsp red wine vinegar
- 1 Tbsp honey
- 1/4 cup of olive oil
- 1 tsp lemon juice
- 1 cup of fresh raspberries

Instructions

1. Everything except the poppy seeds should go into a jar and an immersion blender.
2. Blend until creamy and smooth. You can now strain the mixture to remove the seeds or keep them in. Both of the ways I've made it are fine.
3. Add the poppy seeds and taste, adjusting the seasoning as needed.
4. For up to a week, keep in the refrigerator in an airtight container.

78. COCONUT MILK RANCH DRESSING

Prep Time: 10 Minutes | Cook Time: 00 Minutes

Total Time: 10 Minutes | Serving: 4

Ingredients
- 1/2 cup of mayonnaise
- 1 tsp onion powder
- 1 tsp dried dill
- 2 tsp dried parsley
- 1/4 tsp black pepper
- 1/2 cup of full-fat coconut milk
- 1/2 tsp salt
- 1 tsp apple cider vinegar
- 1 tsp garlic powder
- 1 tbsp dried chives
- 1 green onion
- 1 tsp white wine vinegar

Instructions

1. In a bowl, combine all the ingredients and whisk until thoroughly blended. Use an immersion blender to mix for an exceptionally smooth dressing.
2. Before serving, chill the mixture for at least half an hour after transferring it to a bottle or jar for storage.

79. PITAYA PEACH SMOOTHIE

Prep Time: 10 Minutes | Cook Time: 00 Minutes

Total Time: 10 Minutes | Serving: 11

Ingredients

- ➤ Fresh dragonfruit balls
- ➤ Pinch of sea salt
- ➤ 1/4 tsp Rodelle vanilla extract
- ➤ Handful of ice cubes
- ➤ 1 tbsp golden flaxseed meal
- ➤ Scant 1/4 tsp Rodelle lemon extract
- ➤ 1/3 cup of lightly packed greens
- ➤ 1 frozen dragonfruit pack
- ➤ 1 rounded tbsp almond butter
- ➤ 1 fresh ripe peach
- ➤ 1/3 cup of water
- ➤ 2-3 scoops collagen

Instructions

1. Blend all ingredients in an immersion blender until smooth, adding more liquid as needed. Start by blending the greens with the water for about a minute, then add all the other ingredients and blend again for an even smoother texture.
2. Place a handful of ice and blend again until fully incorporated if you want a smoothie with more ice. Place a fresh dragonfruit balled in a melon baller on top if desired. Serve immediately.

80. PINK POWER STRAWBERRY WATERMELON SMOOTHIE

Prep Time: 10 Minutes | Cook Time: 00 Minutes

Total Time: 10 Minutes | Serving: 6

Ingredients

- ½ medium watermelon chopped
- 200 grams of frozen strawberries
- Juice of 2 lemons
- 60 grams of frozen raspberries
- 1 tbsp raw honey

Instructions

1. Combine the watermelon, strawberries, raspberries, and lemon juice in a large blender. Lend quickly until everything is well combined and silky. If necessary, taste and adjust with more sweetener or lemon juice.
2. Serve right away or store in the fridge for up to a day.

81. PUMPKIN SOUP

Prep Time: 5 Minutes | Cook Time: 20 Minutes

Total Time: 25 Minutes | Serving: 2

Ingredients

- ¼ cup of half and half
- 15 ounces pumpkin puree
- 2 cups of chicken stock
- ⅛ tsp cayenne
- 4 strips bacon
- ¼ tsp nutmeg
- salt and pepper
- ½ tsp rosemary
- 4 cloves garlic
- ½ yellow onion
- 1 apple

Instructions

1. Bring a medium-sized or large pot to a boil.
2. After that, take out the bacon and place it aside. Keep cooking in the same pot as the bacon fat.
3. Add the chopped/peeled apple and onion. Simmer for two to three minutes.
4. Include the garlic. Add the rosemary, cayenne, and nutmeg for seasoning. Simmer for an additional two to three minutes.
5. Combine the stock and pumpkin puree, stirring to combine. Cook for two more minutes or until everything is fragrant and hot.
6. Make sure the soup is perfectly smooth by pureeing it with an immersion blender.
7. Add the cream and stir. Add salt and pepper according to taste.
8. Before serving, chop up the bacon and put it in.

82. WHITE BEAN AND ROSEMARY DIP

Prep Time: 15 Minutes | Cook Time: 00 Minutes

Total Time: 15 Minutes | Serving: 9

Ingredients

- ➢ 2 tsp freshly squeezed lemon juice
- ➢ Pinch of salt and pepper
- ➢ Two 15-ounce cans of cannellini
- ➢ 1 tbsp minced fresh rosemary
- ➢ ¾ to 1 cup of vegetable stock
- ➢ 2 garlic cloves minced

Instructions

1. In a medium-sized saucepan, garlic, heat the vegetable stock, and rosemary over medium-high heat until the ingredients are tender, about 5 minutes. When heated, lower the heat and add the beans.
2. Simmer for 4 to 6 minutes on low heat or until beans are tender. Put the salt, pepper, lemon zest, and juice.
3. Puree for 5 to 10 seconds or until smooth using an immersion blender.
4. Serve immediately or keep chilled for up to four or five days in an airtight container.

83. THAI PEANUT SAUCE

Prep Time: 10 Minutes | Cook Time: 00 Minutes

Total Time: 10 Minutes | Serving: 1

Ingredients

- ➢ 1 Tbsp fresh lime juice
- ➢ 1/2 cup of natural peanut butter
- ➢ 2 Tbsp pure maple syrup
- ➢ 2 Tbsp reduced-sodium gluten-free tamari
- ➢ 3–5 Tbsp light coconut milk

Instructions

1. Mix. Put the peanut butter, 3 Tbsp. Coconut milk, tamari, pure maple syrup, and lime juice in a small bowl or jar.
2. Mix. Add extra coconut milk as necessary to thin the sauce to the right consistency after blending it with an immersion blender until it's smooth and creamy.
3. Put Aside Or Relax. As you cook your chicken, cover and set aside the peanut sauce. If you prepare the peanut sauce, it can be kept in the fridge for up to a week.

84. MASHED CAULIFLOWER

Prep Time: 15 Minutes | Cook Time: 8 Minutes | Total Time: 23 Minutes | Serving: 6

Ingredients

- 1 tsp garlic powder
- ¼ cup of Parmesan cheese
- 1 tsp Olive oil
- 1 medium cauliflower
- Salt and pepper to taste
- 3 tbsp butter melted
- ¼ cup of mayo

Instructions

1. First, add roughly 2 cups of water to a big pot and bring it to a boil.
2. Next, fit a steamer basket into the bottom of the pot.
3. The cauliflower florets should be placed inside the steamer basket.
4. When the cauliflower is soft to the fork, cover the pot and steam it. If you steam the florets for longer than eight minutes, they will get extremely wet.
5. After removing the heat, cover the pot and give the cauliflower five minutes to cool.
6. Once the cauliflower has been steamed, move it to a bowl and seal it with plastic wrap, leaving a small gap for the immersion blender. Mash the cauliflower gradually. It will be difficult to mash at first, but it will get easier quickly. While mashing the steamed cauliflower, do not add any liquid. It will eventually let out a little liquid, making mashing easier. At the end of the process, your mashed cauliflower will become extremely watery if you add more liquid. Add the butter, mayo, Parmesan, garlic powder, salt, and ground black pepper to the smoothed cauliflower and stir until well combined. To adjust the seasoning, taste. Add some olive oil, fresh parsley, and black pepper as garnish.

85. BASIL WALNUT PESTO

Prep Time: 20 Minutes | Cook Time: 10 Minutes | Total Time: 30 Minutes | Serving: 1

Ingredients

- 1/2 cup of Olive oil
- Salt and freshly ground pepper
- 1/2 cup of Walnuts
- 1/2 tsp Lime juice
- 4 Garlic cloves, peeled
- 4 cups of Basil leaves

Instructions

1. Using an immersion blender, combine the walnuts, garlic, basil, salt, and pepper in a jar and blend until a coarse, chunky paste is formed.
2. Olive oil should be added gradually while blending the basil-walnut pesto until smooth. If desired, stir in the lime juice. I enjoy adding a spritz of lime juice because it keeps the color vibrant green and enhances the fresh flavors.
3. Use it as a pasta sauce, over chicken and salmon, or as a spread for sandwiches and salads.

86. CELERIAC AND PARSNIP SOUP

Prep Time: 10 Minutes | Cook Time: 20 Minutes

Total Time: 30 Minutes | Serving: 4

Ingredients

- 1 tbsp maple syrup
- ½ cup of whole milk
- 3 tbsp extra virgin olive oil
- ½ tsp salt
- 3 cloves garlic
- 2.5 cups of diced celeriac
- Parsnip peels
- ¼ tsp pepper
- 4 cups of vegetable broth
- 1 yellow onion
- 12 sage leaves
- 3 cups of sliced parsnips

Instructions

1. For this recipe, use a swivel peeler to peel the parsnips when chopping vegetables, reserving the peels for another time. Before chopping, use a paring knife to peel the celeriac.
2. In a soup pot, preheat 1 tbsp of olive oil over medium heat. When fragrant, add the diced onion and cook for a few minutes. Place the garlic, salt, and pepper and continue cooking for an additional few minutes.
3. Pour the maple syrup, celeriac, and parsnips into the pot. After adding the vegetable broth, turn up the heat so that it boils. Cook, covered, for fifteen minutes on simmering heat until the vegetables are tender.
4. Meanwhile, bring the remaining olive oil to a medium-high temperature in a skillet. Put the sage leaves in a single layer after they're heated. Fry them for 30 to 60 seconds or until they turn crispy. Take out them from the pan and place them on a paper towel-lined plate. When the parsnip peels are crispy, add them to the skillet and cook for a few minutes. Spoon onto the sage-topped plate.
5. Once the soup is cooked through, remove from the heat. Blend using an immersion blender until it's smooth.
6. Spoon soup into bowls; garnish with parsnip peels and crispy sage. Have fun!

87. TOMATO-BASIL SALSA

Prep Time: 5 Minutes | Cook Time: 00 Minutes

Total Time: 5 Minutes | Serving: 16

Ingredients

- ½ cup of fresh basil leaves
- Add red onion
- 4 large Hy-Vee Homegrown tomatoes
- Add Hy-Vee salt
- 1 jalapeno pepper
- Add garlic
- ½ c. red onion
- 3 tbsp. fresh lime juice
- Add fresh lime juice
- Add jalapeno pepper
- 1 tsp. Hy-Vee salt
- 2 clove garlic
- Add fresh basil leaves

Instructions

1. In a 2-quart bowl, mix tomatoes, onion, basil, lime juice, Jalapeno, garlic, and salt.
2. Blend until almost smooth using an immersion blender fitted with the S-blade attachment. After passing the liquid through a fine-mesh sieve, dispose of it. Keep salsa covered and chilled for up to three days.

88. MANGO PINEAPPLE BANANA SMOOTHIE

Prep Time: 5 Minutes | Cook Time: 00 Minutes

Total Time: 5 Minutes | Serving: 1

Ingredients

- 6 ounces of Mango Pulp
- 1 Banana
- Ice Cubes
- 2-3 slices fresh pineapple
- ½ cup of Greek Yogurt

Instructions

1. Peel & cut the fruit flesh from the seed core when using a fresh, whole mango. Remove the banana peel and chop off the pineapple peel.
2. In the blender jar, combine all the fruits, Greek yogurt, and ice cubes; blend until smooth. Alternatively, blend smoothly using an immersion blender fitted with a big, tall plastic jar.
3. Use a reusable straw to serve chilled.

89. CARROT AND CORIANDER SOUP

Prep Time: 5 Minutes | Cook Time: 40 Minutes

Total Time: 45 Minutes | Serving: 4

Ingredients

- ➢ 5 cloves of garlic
- ➢ 1 potato
- ➢ 30 g fresh coriander
- ➢ 1 kg carrots
- ➢ 100 ml double cream
- ➢ 2 onions

Cup board Essentials:

- ➢ 1 litre vegetable stock
- ➢ 3 tbsp extra virgin olive oil
- ➢ 1 tsp dried parsley
- ➢ Salt & Pepper

Instructions

1. Transfer the onions and carrots to a sizable baking sheet. Season with pepper, salt, and dried parsley after adding extra virgin olive oil. Bake for thirty to forty minutes.
2. Add the chopped potato and stock to a large pot after 30 minutes. Preheat the oven to medium and set a ten to fifteen-minute timer.
3. Take the onion and carrots out of the oven when they're ready. After removing the garlic's skin, combine all the ingredients in the pot. After removing the heat, stir in the coriander. Blend with a hand blender until it's smooth.
4. Transfer the cream to the pan and mix thoroughly. After adjusting the seasoning with a taste, serve and savor!

90. BLUEBERRY SMOOTHIE WITH ALMOND BUTTER

Prep Time: 3 Minutes | Cook Time: 00 Minutes

Total Time: 3 Minutes | Serving: 1

Ingredients

- ➢ ½ banana
- ➢ ½ cup of blueberries
- ➢ 1 tbsp cocoa powder
- ➢ ¼ tsp cinnamon
- ➢ 1 tbsp ground flaxseed
- ➢ 6 ounces vanilla soy milk
- ➢ ½ cup of ice chips
- ➢ 1 tbsp almond butter

Instructions

1. Fill the blender cup with all of the ingredients.
2. Blend until smooth, about 10 seconds.

91. ROASTED CELERIAC SOUP

Prep Time: 15 Minutes | Cook Time: 45 Minutes

Total Time: 1 Hour | Serving: 4

Ingredients

- 20 g parsley
- 2 onions
- 1 apple
- 2 tbsp olive oil

- 1 celeriac
- 1 litre vegetable
- ½ lemon
- 2 cloves garlic

To serve:

- fresh herbs

- drizzle cream

Instructions

1. Dice and roast the celeriac first.
2. Chop the garlic and onion coarsely after peeling them.
3. Two garlic cloves, two onions
4. In a medium-sized saucepan with olive oil, saute the onion for a few minutes over medium heat, stirring constantly. The onion should be fragrant, transparent, and have a hint of gold around the edges. Add the garlic and cook for a few more minutes.
5. Two tbsp of olive oil
6. Cut the apple into chunks after cooking it.
7. One apple
8. Season with salt & pepper after adding the roasted celeriac, parsley, apple, and stock to the pan and stirring well. Close the lid and heat to a simmer. After that, immediately reduce the heat to a simmer and let it cook for 20 minutes.
9. 20 grams of parsley, 1 celeriac, and 1 liter of vegetable or chicken stock
10. Once all the vegetables are very soft, puree the soup using an immersion blender.
11. If the soup needs to be thinned, add more stock or taste and adjust the seasoning.
12. Add the lemon juice and stir. Put a knob of butter if you prefer your soup creamier.
13. One-third lemon
14. Top with fresh herbs and a dollop of cream and serve.

92. VEGAN MATCHA ICE CREAM

Prep Time: 15 Minutes | Cook Time: 45 Minutes

Total Time: 1 Hour| Serving: 8

Ingredients

- ➢ 14 ounces Canned Coconut Milk
- ➢ ¼ cup of Golden Syrup
- ➢ 1 tsp Vanilla Extract
- ➢ ½ cup of White Granulated Sugar
- ➢ 1 Tbsp Matcha Green Tea Powder
- ➢ 14 ounces Canned Coconut Cream

Instructions

1. Put your ice cream maker's freezer bowl in the freezer the day before you want to make ice cream to guarantee proper freezing.
2. Next, put your sugar, golden syrup, coconut milk, and coconut cream into a pot and bring it to a simmer while stirring from time to time.
3. After bringing it to a simmer, take it off the burner and mix the matcha green tea powder and vanilla.
4. Blend the mixture in the pot for thirty seconds using an immersion blender. This stage gets rid of any last bits of graininess in your blend. Transfer the mixture to a blender jug. Just be sure to tighten the lid because the mixture will be boiling.
5. After transferring the mixture to a container that can be sealed, refrigerate it for at least one night to allow it to cool fully.
6. After transferring the mixture to your ice cream maker's freezer bowl, stir it until it achieves a soft-serve consistency. This could take anywhere from 20-45 minutes, depending on your ice cream maker.
7. After transferring the ice cream from the ice cream maker to a loaf pan, smooth it down. Before serving, put the foil-covered dish in the freezer to solidify completely.
8. Garnish with chopped pistachios or hazelnuts.

93. CHOCOLATE CHIA PUDDING

Prep Time: 5 Minutes | Cook Time: 00 Minutes

Total Time: 5 Minutes | Serving: 4

Ingredients
- 2 Tbsp maple syrup
- 2 Tbsp cacao powder
- ½ cup of chia seeds
- 1 tsp vanilla extract
- 2 cups of unsweetened almond milk

Instructions

1. Combine almond milk, maple syrup, vanilla, and cacao powder in a bowl or tall measuring cup. You'll need to use some elbow grease to mix the cacao into the liquid until it's thoroughly combined because it will resist stirring. Make use of an immersion blender for optimal results.
2. Stir chia seeds into the mixture of milk. After two to three minutes, stir it, being sure to incorporate all of the seeds into the liquid by scraping down the sides of the bowl.
3. Stir once more after 5 minutes. By now, the chia pudding should have started to thicken and gel as the seeds take in more liquid.
4. Make sure to tightly cover and refrigerate for at least one hour or overnight. Before serving, stir it a good bit.

94. AVOCADO CHOCOLATE MOUSSE

Prep Time: 10 Minutes | Cook Time: 10 Minutes

Total Time: 20 Minutes | Serving: 4

Ingredients
- Salt ½ tsp
- 1 tsp Vanilla Extract
- 3 tbsp Unsweetened Cocoa Powder
- 2 Avocado
- ½ cup of Unsweetened Dark Chocolate Chips
- ¼ cup of Almond Milk

Instructions

1. I explained how to melt chocolate chips in the microwave or stovetop. After taking the chocolate off the stove, let it cool. Meanwhile, blend the remaining ingredients to about a half-blended consistency in a large mixing bowl or with an immersion blender. Once the chocolate has melted, add it and pulse the ingredients until a smooth consistency is achieved. After transferring the mousse to glasses, chill it for at least two hours or until it solidifies. If desired, top with your preferred garnish, such as fruit.

95. CHOCOLATE TRUFFLES

Prep Time: 30 Minutes | Cook Time: 5 Minutes

Total Time: 35 Minutes | Serving: 12

Ingredients

- ➢ 4 ounces heavy whipping cream
- ➢ 8 ounces semi-sweet chocolate

Instructions

1. Chop or shave your chocolate finely.
2. Fill a saucepan with heavy whipping cream. Heat it over medium-low heat until bubbles appear around the edges of the pan.
3. Half the hot cream should be poured into a tall immersion blender cup.
4. Add the chocolate, chopped finely.
5. Cover the chocolate with the leftover heated cream.
6. To allow the chocolate to melt, set it aside for about two minutes.
7. Blend the cream and chocolate using the immersion blender.
8. After scraping down the sides of the cup, pulse the ganache one more until it becomes glossy, smooth, and creamy.
9. Transfer into a shallow bowl, seal it, and leave it for a minimum of four hours.

96. WHOLE WHEAT BLUEBERRY MUFFINS

Prep Time: 10 Minutes | Cook Time: 15 Minutes

Total Time: 25 Minutes | Serving: 12

Ingredients

- 1 tsp Baking Powder
- ½ tsp Baking Soda
- ½ cup of Plant-Based Milk soy
- ⅓ cup of Vegan Powdered Sugar
- 2 Bananas
- 1 ½ cups of Whole Wheat Flour
- ¼ cup of Raw Cane Sugar
- ¾ cup of fresh Blueberries
- 2 tbsp fresh Blueberries
- ¼ cup of Olive Oil
- ¼ tsp Salt

Instructions

1. Set oven temperature to 350 degrees Fahrenheit. A 12-cup of muffin tray should be lined with muffin cups or greased and floured.
2. Using an immersion blender, food processor, or blender, blend bananas, milk, and olive oil until smooth.
3. In a another bowl, mix the sugar, flour, baking soda, baking powder, and salt. Using a wooden spoon, stir the combined wet ingredients after adding them to the bowl.
4. After adding ¾ cup of fresh blueberries, evenly fill muffin cups with muffin mixture.
5. Bake for 15 minutes in the oven. Remove it from the oven and let it cool fully on the cookie rack.
6. In the meantime, mix 2 tbsp fresh blueberries and powdered sugar to make blueberry glaze. After the muffins cool, brush them with glaze and place a blueberry on top.

97. FLUFFY FLOURLESS PANCAKES WITH BANANA

Prep Time: 5 Minutes | Cook Time: 15 Minutesm | Total Time: 20 Minutes | Serving: 6

Ingredients

- 2 large eggs
- 1 tsp ground cinnamon
- 2 ½ cups of milk
- 3 tsp baking powder
- 2 tsp vanilla extract
- 2 large ripe bananas
- 2 heaping tbsp of honey
- 4 cups of old-fashioned rolled oats
- ½ tsp salt

Instructions

1. Put everything into a big bowl. Process everything in an immersion blender until it's very smooth. Or, place all the ingredients in a blender and puree until very smooth.
2. The batter should ideally sit for 15 to 30 minutes to give the oats time to hydrate. Even though I cooked them immediately, the pancakes became fluffier and better after sitting. Thus, simply sit, sip your coffee.
3. Over medium heat, preheat a large nonstick pan. When it's hot, grease the skillet with butter, coconut oil, or oil, then transfer the batter onto it. Simmer each side for two to three minutes.

98. COCONUT SORBET

Prep Time: 20 Minutes | Cook Time: 00 Minutes | Total Time: 20 Minutes | Serving: 10

Ingredients

- 1 can coconut cream
- 1 can coconut milk
- 1 cup of coconut water
- 1 cup of granulated sugar
- ½ cup of sweetened shredded coconut
- 1 tsp coconut extract

Instructions

1. In a small saucepan, combine the sugar and coconut water and heat over medium heat until the sugar dissolves. Once the sugar is dissolved, pour the simple syrup into a jar and keep it chilled for at least eight hours or overnight. Refrigerate the cream and coconut milk as well. Freeze the ice cream bowl until it solidifies.
2. Blend the coconut milk, coconut cream, and coconut water together until smooth.
3. When the mixture starts to ice but is still very soft, add it to an ice cream maker and churn for 15-20 minutes. If using, add the coconut extract in the final minute.
4. If you're using shredded coconut, fold it in after removing the insert and scraping off any sorbet.
5. After transferring the sorbet, seal a freezer-safe container. For at least three hours, freeze.
6. After 10 minutes of room temperature sorbet sitting, scoop and serve.

99. STRAWBERRY BASIL LEMONADE

Prep Time: 5 Minutes | Cook Time: 00 Minutes

Total Time: 5 Minutes | Serving: 4

Ingredients

- 10 lemons
- ¾ cup of superfine sugar
- ⅓ cup of fresh basil
- 8-10 strawberries
- 4 cups of warm water
- ½ cup of vodka optional

Instructions

1. After the lemons have been juiced, pour the juice into a big pitcher.
2. Stir to mix and dissolve the sugar after adding the water and sugar. Allow to cool completely.
3. Stir in the basil and strawberries.
4. Blend the mixture for about 20 seconds, or until it turns pink and the basil is finely chopped, using an immersion blender. If you wish, strain out any infused basil pieces into the beverage.
5. If desired, add alcohol. Enjoy it served over crushed ice!

100. PEAR ICE CREAM

Prep Time: 20 Minutes | Cook Time: 25 Minutes

Total Time: 45 Minutes | Serving: 6

Ingredients

- ➤ 2 cups of thickened cream
- ➤ 2 tsp tapioca starch
- ➤ ½ tbsp glucose syrup
- ➤ 2 tbsp unsalted butter
- ➤ 2 to 3 tsp ground ginger
- ➤ 4 medium very ripe pears
- ➤ ½ cup of tightly packed brown sugar

Instructions

1. Dice, peel and core the pears.
2. Put the brown sugar and butter into a frying pan or skillet. Stirring frequently, cook over medium heat until butter and sugar are melted and foamy.
3. Stir thoroughly after adding the diced pears. Stir well and cook for a few minutes with the pears. A lot of juice will come out of the pears.
4. Stirring frequently, continue cooking the pears for about twenty minutes or until they have cooked to a beautiful, thick, almost jammy consistency.
5. Let cool before transferring to a deep-sided jug that can be used with an immersion blender. Process until the pears are smooth, then strain. One and a half cups of pureed pear should be available.
6. Pour the cream into a tiny pot. Combine the two tbsp of cream and the tapioca starch in a small bowl, stirring to blend. When the cream is slightly heated, and the glucose syrup has completely dissolved, add the glucose syrup and stir.
7. Add the tapioca starch slurry to the warm cream mixture and thoroughly mix. Take off the heat source. If you have trouble blending in the tapioca starch, use an immersion blender to quickly and carefully blitz the mixture.
8. Incorporate the cream mixture thoroughly into the strained pears. For at least four hours, preferably overnight, cover and refrigerate.
9. To chill, place your storage container in the freezer. Take the churning bowl out of the freezer just before if you're using a self-refrigerating ice cream churner; if not, turn it on about ten minutes beforehand.
10. Beat the frozen yogurt. When finished, it will have a soft-serve consistency. Once solid, cover and freeze for a minimum of four hours.
11. Take out from the freezer, scoop, and serve. Delicious either by itself or paired with my simple pear compote. Delicious!

101. STRAWBERRY ICE CREAM

Prep Time: 10 Minutes | Cook Time: 00 Minutes

Total Time: 10 Minutes | Serving: 3

Ingredients

- 1 tbsp vodka
- ¼ tsp xanthan gum
- 2 tbsp low-calorie natural sweetener
- ⅓ cup of chopped strawberries
- 1 tsp vanilla extract
- 1 cup of heavy whipping cream
- 1 pinch salt

Instructions

1. In a wide-mouth pint-sized jar, combine heavy cream, strawberries, sweetener, vodka, vanilla extract, xanthan gum, and salt.
2. Blend the cream mixture for 60 to 75 seconds, or until soft peaks have formed and thickened, using an immersion blender and an up-and-down motion.
3. After 3 to 4 hours, or until the ice cream reaches the desired consistency, cover the jar and freeze, stirring every 30 to 40 minutes.

Made in the USA
Las Vegas, NV
02 November 2024

11030934R00052